O'REILLY®
Strata
Making Data Work

Learn ho
data into

T0260815

From startups to the Fortune 500, smart companies are betting on data-driven insight, seizing the opportunities that are emerging from the convergence of four powerful trends:

- New methods of collecting, managing, and analyzing data

- Cloud computing that offers inexpensive storage and flexible, on-demand computing power for massive data sets

- Visualization techniques that turn complex data into images that tell a compelling story

- Tools that make the power of data available to anyone

Get control over big data and turn it into insight with O'Reilly's Strata offerings. Find the inspiration and information to create new products or revive existing ones, understand customer behavior, and get the data edge.

Visit oreilly.com/data to learn more.

Designing Data Visualizations

Noah Iliinsky and Julie Steele

O'REILLY®

Beijing · Cambridge · Farnham · Köln · Sebastopol · Tokyo

Designing Data Visualizations

by Noah Iliinsky and Julie Steele

Copyright © 2011 Julie Steele and Noah Iliinsky. All rights reserved.
Printed in the United States of America.

Published by O'Reilly Media, Inc., 1005 Gravenstein Highway North, Sebastopol, CA 95472.

O'Reilly books may be purchased for educational, business, or sales promotional use. Online editions are also available for most titles (*http://my.safaribooksonline.com*). For more information, contact our corporate/institutional sales department: (800) 998-9938 or *corporate@oreilly.com*.

Editor: Julie Steele
Production Editor: Teresa Elsey

Cover Designer: Karen Montgomery
Interior Designer: David Futato
Illustrator: Robert Romano

Revision History for the First Edition:

See *http://oreilly.com/catalog/errata.csp?isbn=9781449312282* for release details.

ISBN: 978-1-449-31228-2

[LSI]

1321996768

Table of Contents

Part II.   How Should You Design It?

Preface

The path from journeyman to master is long. In the case of data visualization, the path has been well marked by many accomplished designers and cognitive scientists who have been doing great work for decades. We gladly follow in their footsteps, and we hope you will, too.

In these pages, however, our goal is not so much to take you to the summit as to start you down the path—and that the path is quite rewarding to travel. Our goal is to give you confidence as you begin your journey.

Many statisticians and practitioners with excellent coding and data munging skills are nevertheless stuck in a rut of common formats and default settings, which lead to mundane, suboptimal visualizations. But the domain of hand-crafted, fine-tuned, noteworthy visualizations is not limited to "creative" types; it is accessible with a bit of guidance.

The truth is, there *is* plenty of room for artistry and creativity in data visualization. But success is built upon a linear process that encodes information for visual transmission and subsequent decoding by wetware—the reader's brain. One aim in writing this book is to introduce you to this process, including some basic concepts and best practices, so that your message may be transmitted with minimal interference.

It *is* a process. And design is something you're probably already doing, whether you're designing applications, frameworks, graphics, or something else. Design is simply a process of organized thinking, planning, and executing. You are making design choices, intentional or not. Of course, intentional choices have a better chance of being useful than arbitrary or accidental choices.* This book is a road map to those choices: it is meant to make you aware of the choices you get to make, and to help you make useful, intentional design decisions at every turn.

This high-level road map is one we haven't seen presented anywhere else. It will give you the general lay of the land. It is a set of steps and rules to follow that will get you 80% of the way to turning out great work. We'll introduce many questions you'll need to ask yourself, and point you in the direction of some answers. The nuanced details

---

* Suh: *The Principles of Design* (Oxford University Press); Schon: *The Reflective Practitioner* (Basic Books).

of those answers have already been addressed by others, and we hope you will continue down the path with further guidance from our colleagues and mentors (see the Reading List in Appendix A).

Note that Appendix A also covers some of the many tools available for creating data visualizations, and we hope you will peruse them. But you'll find a discussion of tools intentionally missing from the rest of the book, because the topic at hand is, "What problem are you solving?" (and the questions you're answering), rather than, "What tools are you using?" Design and implementation are two separate things.

As in any creative discipline, the best data visualizations are forged by breaking some of the rules. But rules must be broken with intention. One must learn the rules (well, more like guidelines) before one is entitled to break them. With that in mind, we present for your consideration our process for the visual encoding of information.

How This Book Is Organized

This book is organized into two major parts, which can loosely be thought of as practical theoretical foundations and applied suggestions, respectively.

In Part I, we discuss different kinds of visualization (including infographics and visual art) and explore the influences at work in each one. The goal is to help you become a more savvy consumer of visualizations, as well as a more organized thinker when creating your own visual work.

In Chapter 1, we introduce some ways of classifying and describing different styles of visualization, so that you can begin to think about and describe what you're designing.

In Chapter 2, we introduce the three fundamental influences to the visualization product—the designer, the reader, and the data—and describe how each should shape what is eventually created.

In Part II, we apply these concepts to the design process. The goal is to help you think in a linear way about how to select and apply appropriate encodings for your data.

In Chapter 3, we focus on getting to a clear understanding of your goals—and defining the requisite supporting data—so that you can implement them most effectively.

In Chapter 4, we lay out heuristics for understanding the shape of your data and choosing compatible visual properties and structures with which to encode it.

In Chapter 5, we dive deep into the property of *spatial position*—axes and placement—one of the most important properties you'll need to select. We also discuss using different visualization structures.

In Chapter 6, we look at best practices and offer specific suggestions for encoding many specific different data types with visual properties. We also present warnings against common pitfalls and dark patterns.

Finally, the Appendices are full of resources and references meant to help you put your skills into practice and expand your knowledge beyond this volume.

Appendix A contains a list of tools to help you get started, as well as a suggested reading list to expand your knowledge and understanding of design concepts.

Appendix B is a list of the questions and decisions you'll confront as part of the design process. We hope you'll read the entire book, and then use this section as a refresher whenever you design a new visualization.

What We Mean When We Say...

In this book, we'll use some specific terms to describe your data and visual encodings. Here is a handy glossary for quick reference.

Chart: Something that shows qualitative information (e.g., flow charts).

Data dimensions: One single channel of data. A stock graph may comprise four properties: date, price, company, and market cap. Each is a unique dimension of the data, which can be encoded separately, with a different visual property.

Data visualization: Visualizations that are algorithmically generated and can be easily regenerated with different data, are usually data-rich, and are often aesthetically shallow.

Designer: The creator of a visualization; any reader of this book.

Encoding: The visual property (noun) applied to a dimension of data that *encodes* (verb) the information into a visual medium for decoding by the reader's brain.

Explanatory visualization: Data visualizations that are used to transmit information or a point of view from the designer to the reader. Explanatory visualizations typically have a specific "story" or information that they are intended to transmit.

Exploratory visualization: Data visualizations that are used by the designer for self-informative purposes to discover patterns, trends, or sub-problems in a dataset. Exploratory visualizations typically don't have an already-known story.

Graph: Something that shows quantitative information (e.g., pie graphs and bar graphs).

Infographic: Visualizations that are manually generated around specific data, tend to be data-shallow, and are often aesthetically rich.

Reader: The consumer of a visualization, often someone other than the designer. The reader has information needs that are meant to be satisfied by the visualization.

Visual property: A characteristic that you can see. Color, size, location, thickness, and line weight are all visual properties.

Variability of a property or data dimension: Within a visual property or single data dimension, what values are present or allowed, and how they change. Integers vary discretely; position can vary continuously. Categories are finite (and discrete, though maybe hierarchical); numbers are infinite.

Figures Used by Permission

The following figures are reprinted by kind permission:

Figure 1-3. Flint Hahn (2010). Copyright © 2010, Flint Hahn. Permission to reproduce the likeness of Burning Man and the mark "Burning Man" granted by Burning Man.

Figure 1-5. Nora Ligorano and Marshall Reese (2011). Copyright © 2011, Ligorano/Reese. *http://ligoranoreese.net/fiber-optic-tapestry*

Figure 4-1. European Soil Bureau. Copyright © 1995–2011, European Union. Used with stated authorization to reproduce, with acknowledgment. *http://eusoils.jrc.ec.eu ropa.eu/*

Figure 4-2. Center for International Earth Science Information Network (CIESIN) (2007). Copyright © 2007, The Trustees of Columbia University in the City of New York. Columbia University. Population, Landscape, and Climate Estimates (PLACE). Used under the Creative Commons Attribution License. *http://sedac.ciesin.columbia .edu/place/*

Figure 4-5. Tableau Software Public Gallery. Copyright © 2003–2011 Tableau Software. *http://www.tableausoftware.com/learn/gallery/company-performance*

Figure 4-6. Christian Caron (2011). Copyright © 2011, Christian Caron.

Figure 4-10. Michael Dayah (1997). Copyright © 1997 Michael Dayah. *http://www .ptable.com*

Figure 4-15. Robert Palmer (2010). Copyright © 2010, Robert Palmer. *http://rp-network .com/*

Figure 5-1 and Figure 5-2. Photo credits to: Annette Crimmins, Sias van Schalkwyk, Janni Due, Dimitri Castrique, and Grethe Boe.

Figure 5-6. Nelson Minar (2011). Copyright © 2011 Daedalus Bits, LLC. *http://wind history.com/*

Figure 5-7. Craig Robinson (2011). Copyright © 2011, Craig Robinson. *http://www .flipflopflyin.com/flipflopflyball/info-majorleagueparks.html*

Figure 5-8. Tableau Software Public Gallery. Copyright © 2003–2011 Tableau Software. *http://www.tableausoftware.com/learn/gallery/federal-stimulus-cost*

Figure 6-3. Spective® Colour System is the evolved color selection method created by Tony Scauzillo-Golden in 2010 while improving upon existing design industry standard color UIs. Please visit TSG's Spective Productions website (*http://www.spectivepro .com*) for further details. Spective® is registered under United States Patent Reg. No. 3,896,334.

Figure 6-11. Jess Bachman (2011). Copyright © 2011, Jess Bachman. *http://www.smar ter.org/research/apples-to-oranges/*

See the Color Figures Online

The images in this book were designed to be viewed in color and at full size. If you're reading the print edition or on a mobile device, please download the color figures from the website for this book (*http://examples.oreilly.com/9781449312282/*) to see them in their full glory.

Attributions and Permissions

This book is here to help you get your job done. If you reference limited parts of it in your work or writings, we appreciate, but do not require, attribution. An attribution usually includes the title, author, publisher, and ISBN. For example: "*Designing Data Visualizations* by Noah Iliinsky and Julie Steele (O'Reilly). Copyright 2011 Julie Steele and Noah Iliinsky, 978-1-449-31228-2."

If you feel your use of examples or quotations from this book falls outside fair use or the permission given above, feel free to contact us at *permissions@oreilly.com*.

Safari® Books Online

 Safari Books Online is an on-demand digital library that lets you easily search over 7,500 technology and creative reference books and videos to find the answers you need quickly.

With a subscription, you can read any page and watch any video from our library online. Read books on your cell phone and mobile devices. Access new titles before they are available for print, and get exclusive access to manuscripts in development and post feedback for the authors. Copy and paste code samples, organize your favorites, download chapters, bookmark key sections, create notes, print out pages, and benefit from tons of other time-saving features.

O'Reilly Media has uploaded this book to the Safari Books Online service. To have full digital access to this book and others on similar topics from O'Reilly and other publishers, sign up for free at *http://my.safaribooksonline.com*.

How to Contact Us

Please address comments and questions concerning this book to the publisher:

O'Reilly Media, Inc.
1005 Gravenstein Highway North
Sebastopol, CA 95472
800-998-9938 (in the United States or Canada)
707-829-0515 (international or local)
707-829-0104 (fax)

We have a web page for this book, where we list errata, examples, and any additional information. You can access this page at:

http://www.oreilly.com/catalog/9781449312282

To comment or ask technical questions about this book, send email to:

bookquestions@oreilly.com

For more information about our books, courses, conferences, and news, see our website at *http://www.oreilly.com*.

Find us on Facebook: *http://facebook.com/oreilly*

Follow us on Twitter: *http://twitter.com/oreillymedia*

Watch us on YouTube: *http://www.youtube.com/oreillymedia*

Acknowledgments

We wish to thank all the amazing visual thinkers and designers who came before us, who work with us, who inspire us. Many of them are cited in the Reading List in Appendix A, and many others have kindly given us permission to reprint their work here. We also wish to thank the good folks at O'Reilly who helped this project come to life.

In particular, Noah would like to thank professor David Farkas, as one of the many origins of this book can be traced to Dave's suggestion to "take a quarter and look at some diagrams, and see what happens," many years ago.

Finally, big thanks and hugs to our friends, and especially our family members, who have loved, supported, fed, and encouraged us over the hectic writing period. Martin, Miller, Amy, Juliebot WCE, Nathan, Noël, Tanya, Edd, and Anna: thanks for keeping us going and for cheering us on.

PART I

What Will You Design?

Since you are interested in learning more about designing data visualizations (by virtue of the fact that you're reading this book), then chances are good that you have been the reader of other people's data visualizations. You may already understand—intuitively or consciously—some of the visual techniques that work well, and some that don't. You may also be aware of some of the different categories of visualization.

The first part of this book aims to help you build your understanding of these categories and techniques. We will explain how to recognize and think about them, so that you will be better prepared to discuss, plan, and consume all kinds of data visualizations.

Why Visualization?

Before we dive into the categories, however, it may be useful to pause for a moment and be explicit about why visualization is a useful medium for examining, understanding, and transmitting information.

- Visualization leverages the incredible capabilities and bandwidth of the visual system to move a huge amount of information into the brain very quickly.
- Visualization takes advantage of our brains' built-in "software" to identify patterns and communicate relationships and meaning.
- Visualization can inspire new questions and further exploration.
- Visualization helps identify sub-problems.
- Visualization is really good for identifying trends and outliers, discovering or searching for interesting or specific data points in a larger field, etc.

The key function of data visualization is to move information from point A to point B. In *exploratory visualization*, point A is the dataset and point B is the designer's own mind. In *explanatory visualization*, point A is the mind of the designer, and point B is the mind of the reader. (More about these categories in Chapter 1.) In order to cross the gulf between points A and B and be successfully communicated, the information must be encoded for transmission. In this case, visual elements are the chosen transmission medium.

For this reason, the designer's purpose in designing a data visualization is to create a deliverable that will be well received and easily understood by the reader. All design choices and particular implementations must serve this purpose.

CHAPTER 1

Classifications of Visualizations

There are several ways to categorize and think about different kinds of visualizations. Here are four of the most useful. The first two are unrelated to the others; the last two are related to each other.

Complexity

One way to classify a data visualization is by counting how many different *data dimensions* it represents. By this we mean the number of discrete types of information that are visually encoded in a diagram. For example, a simple line graph may show the *price* of a company's stock on different *days*: that's two data dimensions. If multiple *companies* are shown (and therefore compared), there are now three dimensions; if *trading volume* per day is added to the graph, there are four (Figure 1-1).

This count of the number of data dimensions can be described as the level of *complexity* of the visualization. As visualizations become more complex, they are more challenging to design well, and can be more difficult to learn from. For that reason, visualizations with no more than three or four dimensions of data are the most common—though visualizations with six, seven, or more dimensions can be found.

 Adding more volume or data points of the same data dimension doesn't increase complexity. Showing 100 years of stock data for one stock isn't more complex than one week of data, it's just more voluminous. Showing 50 companies instead of two might make the display more crowded or complicated, but fundamentally it's just more data points in the company dimension, and therefore isn't making the graph more complex.

There are two main challenges to designing more complex visualizations. The first is that the more dimensions you need to encode visually, the more individual visual properties you need to use. Selecting properties is easy to do for the first few dimensions when most visual properties haven't been used. However, as more dimensions are

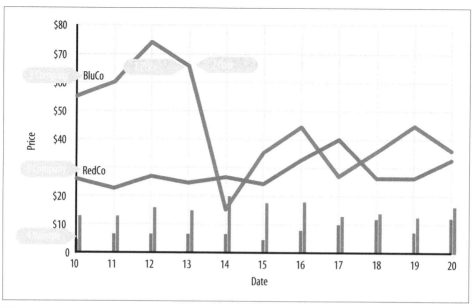

Figure 1-1. Four data dimensions are shown in this graph. Adding more points within any of these dimensions won't change the graph's complexity.

added, finding appropriate, unused visual properties becomes more difficult. (Bear in mind that a visualization shows not just types of information but also the *relationships* between and among those information types.) As this difficulty in design increases, intentionality in the decision-making process becomes ever more necessary.

The way to succeed in the face of this challenge is to be intentional about which property to use for each dimension, and iterate or change encodings as the design evolves. This is the subject of Part II.

The second challenge for designing more complex visualizations is that there are relatively few well-known conventions, metaphors, defaults, and best practices to rely on. Because the safety net of convention may not exist, there is more of a burden on the designer to make good choices that can be easily understood by the reader.

Infographics versus Data Visualization

You may have heard the terms *infographics* and *data visualization* used in different ways, or interchangeably in different contexts, or even casually by the same person in a single sentence. You may also have heard these terms used politically—that is, with positive or negative connotations attached. Some people use *infographic* to refer to representations of information perceived as casual, funny, or frivolous, and *visualization* to refer to designs perceived to be more serious, rigorous, or academic.

The truth is, even though the art of representing statistical information visually is hundreds of years old, the vocabulary of the field is still evolving and settling. Among the general public, there is still confusion over what these two terms mean, but within the information design community, definitions for these terms are solidifying.

In short: The distinction between *infographics* and *data visualizations* (or *information visualizations*) is based on both form and origin (see Figure 1-2).

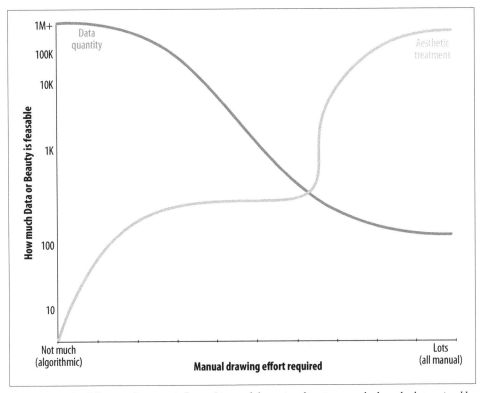

Figure 1-2. The difference between infographics and data visualization may be loosely determined by the method of generation, the quantity of data represented, and the degree of aesthetic treatment applied.

Infographics

We suggest that the term *infographics* is useful for referring to any visual representation of data that is:

- manually drawn (and therefore a custom treatment of the information);
- specific to the data at hand (and therefore nontrivial to recreate with different data);
- aesthetically rich (strong visual content meant to draw the eye and hold interest); and

- relatively data-poor (because each piece of information must be manually encoded).

Put another way, infographics are illustrations where the data representation is manually laid out or sketched, probably with drawing software such as Adobe Illustrator. Because of their manually-drawn process of creation, infographics have the option of being aesthetically rich (see Figure 1-3*). Another consequence of their manual origins is they tend to be limited in the amount of data they can convey, simply due to the practical limitations of manipulating many data points. Similarly, it is difficult to change or update the data in an infographic, as any changes must be implemented manually.

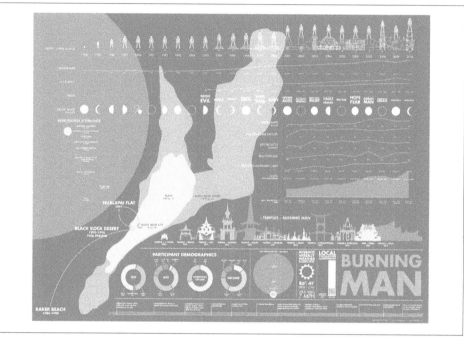

Figure 1-3. Flint Hahn's Burning Man infographic is a great example of an aesthetically rich, manually-drawn piece.

This is not a complete, universal, or absolute definition, but may be a helpful way to think about and identify the category.

Data Visualization

By contrast, we suggest that the terms *data visualization* and *information visualization* (casually, *data viz* and *info viz*) are useful for referring to any visual representation of data that is:

- algorithmically drawn (may have custom touches but is largely rendered with the help of computerized methods);
- easy to regenerate with different data (the same form may be repurposed to represent different datasets with similar dimensions or characteristics);
- often aesthetically barren (data is not decorated); and
- relatively data-rich (large volumes of data are welcome and viable, in contrast to infographics).

Data visualizations are initially designed by a human, but are then drawn algorithmically with graphing, charting, or diagramming software. The advantage of this approach is that it is relatively simple to update or regenerate the visualization with more or new data. While they may show great volumes of data, information visualizations are often less aesthetically rich than infographics.

 As you will have inferred from the title of this book, it is this latter category of data visualizations with which we are primarily concerned here. However, the principles we present *are* relevant to the design of both infographics and data visualizations.

Exploration versus Explanation

Generally speaking, there are two categories of data visualization: *exploration* and *explanation*. The two serve different purposes, and so there are tools and approaches that may be appropriate only for one and not the other. For this reason, it is important to understand the distinction, so that you can be sure you are using tools and approaches appropriate to the task at hand.

Exploration

Exploratory data visualizations are appropriate when you have a whole bunch of data and you're *not sure what's in it*. When you need to get a sense of what's inside your data set, translating it into a visual medium can help you quickly identify its features, including interesting curves, lines, trends, or anomalous outliers.

Exploration is generally best done at a high level of granularity. There may be a whole lot of noise in your data, but if you oversimplify or strip out too much information, you could end up missing something important. This type of visualization is typically part of the *data analysis* phase, and is used to find *the story the data has to tell you*.

Explanation

By contrast, explanatory data visualization is appropriate when you already know what the data has to say, and you are *trying to tell that story to somebody else*. It could be the head of your department, a grant committee, or the general public.

Whoever your audience is, the story you are trying to tell (or the answer you are trying to share) is *known to you at the outset*, and therefore you can design to specifically accommodate and highlight that story. In other words, you'll need to make certain *editorial decisions* about which information stays in, and which is distracting or irrelevant and should come out. This is a process of selecting focused data that will support the story you are trying to tell.

If exploratory data visualization is part of the data analysis phase, then explanatory data visualization is part of the presentation phase. Such a visualization may stand on its own, or *may be part of a larger presentation*, such as a speech, a newspaper article, or a report. In these scenarios, there is some supporting narrative—written or verbal—that further explains things.

Hybrids: Exploratory Explanation

It's worth noting that there is also a kind of hybrid category, which involves a *curated dataset* that is nonetheless presented with the intention to allow some exploration on the reader's part. These visualizations are usually interactive via some kind of graphical interface that lets the reader choose and constrain certain parameters, thereby discovering for herself whatever insights the dataset may have to offer. These might even be insights the creator of the visualization hasn't come across yet.

So in these hybrid designs there is a certain freedom-of-discovery aspect to the information presented, but it is usually not totally raw; it has been distilled and facilitated to some extent. See *http://www.juiceanalytics.com/nfl-visualization/* for an example.

Informative versus Persuasive versus Visual Art

We posit that there are three main categories of explanatory visualizations based on the relationships between the three necessary players: the designer, the reader, and the data.

This section refers to explanatory (or hybrid) visualizations exclusively, because it discusses designing visualizations of data with known parameters and stories. If you don't yet know the message you intend to convey, then you're still in an exploration phase, and probably aren't designing for the same styles of consumption as this section describes.

The Designer-Reader-Data Trinity

It is useful to think of an effective explanatory data visualization as being supported by a three-legged stool consisting of the designer, the reader, and the data. Each of these "legs" exerts a force, or contributes a separate perspective, that must be taken into consideration for a visualization to be stable and successful. Chapter 2 will address the considerations of each of the three in much more detail, but we find it helpful to introduce the concept here.

Each of the three legs of the stool has a unique relationship to the other two. While it is necessary to account for the needs and perspective of all three in each visualization project, the dominant relationship will ultimately determine which category of visualization is needed (see Figure 1-4).

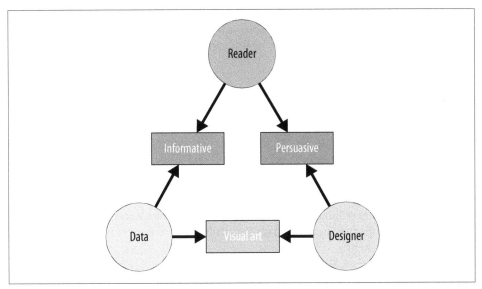

Figure 1-4. The nature of the visualization depends on which relationship (between two of the three components) is dominant.

Informative

An *informative visualization* primarily serves the relationship *between the reader and the data*. It aims for a neutral presentation of the facts in such a way that will educate the reader (though not necessarily persuade him). Informative visualizations are often associated with broad data sets, and seek to distill the content into a manageably consumable form. Ideally, they form the bulk of visualizations that the average person encounters on a day-to-day basis—whether that's at work, in the newspaper, or on a service-provider's website. The Burning Man Infographic (Figure 1-2) is an example of informative visualization.

Persuasive

A *persuasive visualization* primarily serves the relationship *between the designer and the reader*. It is useful when the designer wishes to change the reader's mind about something. It represents a very specific point of view, and advocates a change of opinion or action on the part of the reader. In this category of visualization, the data represented is specifically chosen for the purpose of supporting the designer's point of view, and is presented carefully so as to convince the reader of same. See also: *propaganda*.

 While an informative visualization may not have an intentional point of view in the manner that a persuasive visualization does, all visualizations are going to be biased to some degree, based on the fact that designers are human and have to make choices.

A good example of persuasive visualization is the Joint Economic Committee minority's rendition of the proposed Democratic health care plan in 2010, shown in Figure 4-14.

Visual Art

The third category, *visual art*, primarily serves the relationship *between the designer and the data*. Visual art is unlike the previous two categories in that it often entails *unidirectional* encoding of information, meaning that the reader may not be able to decode the visual presentation to understand the underlying information.

Whereas both informative and persuasive visualizations are meant to be easily decodable—*bidirectional* in their encoding—visual art merely translates the data into a visual form. The designer may intend only to condense it, translate it into a new medium, or make it beautiful; she may not intend for the reader to be able to extract anything from it other than enjoyment.

This category of visualization is sometimes more easily recognized than others. For example, Nora Ligorano and Marshall Reese designed a project that converts Twitter streams into a woven fiber-optic tapestry (Figure 1-5[†]; *http://ligoranoreese.net/fiber-op tic-tapestry*). A project like this is abstract enough that most people intuitively recognize it as art: something to be appreciated rather than explicitly decoded.

But a project like the Planetary app from Bloom Studios (*http://planetary.bloom.io/*) is less easily categorized. Ostensibly, one may decode the information represented visually by noting the number of stars (representing artists), planets (representing albums), and moons (representing tracks) in a constellation or galaxy on the screen. But properties such as track length, encoded as the speed at which the each moon orbits its album-planet, are encoded too subtly for the average user to decode—at which point,

† Nora Ligorano and Marshall Reese (2011). Copyright © 2011, Ligorano/Reese. *http://ligoranoreese.net/fiber -optic-tapestry*

it just becomes something pretty to look at. A worthy pursuit in its own right, perhaps, but better clearly labeled as visual art, and not confused with informative visualization.

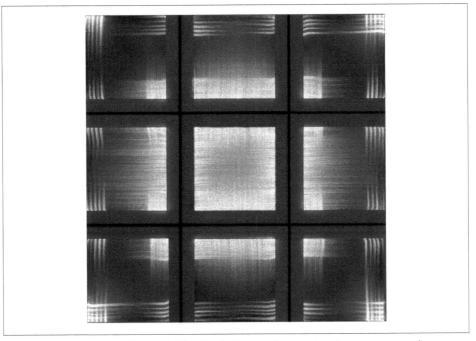

Figure 1-5. Participants address the Fiber Optic Tapestry by tweeting #optictapestry and a primary color—the tapestry displays the colors in algorithmically-determined patterns.

CHAPTER 2

Source Trinity: Ingredients of Successful Visualizations

Let's look a little more closely at the three major sources of influence on the design of your data visualization. It's important to be clear that this applies mainly to *explanatory* visualization. While *exploratory* visualization is more about you finding out what's in your data, explanatory visualization is about you as a *designer* telling the story of the *data* to your *reader*. These three components are your holy trinity when designing data visualizations.

Designer

As a designer, you have a goal. You may not be aware of it, but you are creating a visualization *for some reason*. Being aware of your motivations, goals, and priorities will help you *design* a successful visualization, rather than merely create an arbitrary visual representation of your data.

Why Are You Here?

Understanding and defining your goal is key to your success; it is the foundation of your process. Having a well-defined goal will inform your subsequent design decisions, and will give you a standard to evaluate your design against. And it will help you make appropriate choices long before you start assigning axes and plotting points.

As discussed in Chapter 1, there are different types of visualizations. Knowing which type of visualization you're working with is an excellent first step in your design process. You need to know whether you have a specific story to tell with your data (explanation), or you are visualizing it to begin to see what's there (exploration). If you have a story to tell, your visualization is almost certainly informative, persuasive, or visual art.

Once you know what type of visualization you're creating, you can begin thinking about what kind of experience that visualization type should provide to your reader (even if that's you). What information should they be able to learn from this visualization? What point or message are you trying to convey? (Of course, if your piece is primarily meant to be an artistic work, your goal may be all about aesthetics, not information, and we would not presume to tell you how to make art.)

Keep your goal in mind. It is your touchstone, your guiding light. Consult it when you are about to be seduced by the siren song of circular layouts, the allure of extra data, the false prophet of "because I can." These are distractions on your journey. As Bruce Lee would say, "It is like a finger pointing a way to the moon. Don't concentrate on the finger or you will miss all that heavenly glory."*

To be clear, you should be open to iteration and evolution, serendipity, and the paths that new insight may reveal. But never lose sight of why you're here in the first place. Your unique perspective is the value you bring to the table, and it should inform your design choices.

Reader

The second source of influence is the reader. As the intended recipient of your ideas, the reader holds a very special place in the trinity and can be your biggest ally or your biggest hurdle in clear communication—sometimes both.

You Are Creating This for Other People

At all stages of creating your visualization, it is important to put yourself in the shoes of your reader, and to take into consideration the unique viewpoint that he will bring with him.

Why? *Your success is measured by your reader's success.*

Remember, explanatory data visualization is a communication medium. You are selectively encoding specific information in such a way that the reader will be able to decode it and successfully receive your message. If that message is misinterpreted or poorly received, then you have not done a very good job of encoding it, have you? In order to be successful, you need to consider the various "distortions" or filters your readers will introduce.

Another benefit to putting yourself in the reader's shoes is that it will force you to simplify your explanations a bit. This is *not* the same as simplifying your ideas. It's merely a process of breaking down those ideas until you can communicate them in clear and transparent terms.

If you find that you can't explain your data or your thinking in a straightforward manner, it might be because you yourself don't understand them well enough, or haven't

---

* *http://www.youtube.com/watch?v=sDW6vkuqGLg*

thought enough about a logical way to present them. This process can be a learning opportunity for you, too, and may ultimately strengthen your research.

They Are Not You

At the risk of stating the obvious, it's important to note that your audience is not you. That is to say: if we agree that the purpose of the visualization is to take a story that is already known to you and tell it to somebody else, then it stands to reason that the somebody else is exactly that—not you, but an *other*.

Your grandmother, your boss, your niece, your neighbor—all these people bring different contexts to the table. And that doesn't even begin to cover questions like, "What is the reader's political identity and how do I characterize the borders between countries?" *Your audience is not like you.* Even if you are creating a visualization for your team at work or for others in your own demographic group, you have the "curse" of too much knowledge, which lets you make too many assumptions.

For this reason, you must learn how to take yourself out of the picture when assessing how your message will be received.[†] We acknowledge: this is difficult to do! (But the payoff will be worth it in the end.)

Contextual Considerations for the Reader

Think of throwing a plastic disc with a friend in the park. If you want to be successful, you won't just drop the disk on the ground in the same spot where you are standing: you will exert some physical effort to toss it to where your friend can reach it. Further, if you are an experienced disc-tosser, you will, consciously or not, take into account considerations like how long your friend's arms are, whether she is already in motion and, if so, in which direction she is moving, and how fast.

Effective communication is just like that. Your own position matters, but it is not the same—and does not matter nearly as much—as the position of your receiver, whether they are receiving a plastic disc or a dataset.

The considerations you'll need to make when designing a data visualization, then, are questions of identity, motivation, and language (i.e., specialized knowledge and vocabulary, such as professional jargon).

Another thing to consider is learned social context. This encompasses questions such as:

- What do colors mean?
- Which direction it the reader used to reading in?
- Which icons is she familiar with?

---

† The ability to do this will help you in lots of other areas of your life, too.

We'll take a closer look at how certain reader contexts affect encoding choices for attributes such as titles, tags, and labels; colors; and directional orientation in "Readers' Context" on page 31.

Context of Use

To extend the plastic disc metaphor, a successful toss takes into consideration not only the attributes your friend possesses (arm-length, motion, speed), but also the attributes of the context surrounding your friend: things like whether the wind is blowing, whether the sun is in her eyes, and whether the terrain is even.

Similarly, a successful data visualization will take into account different time-frames the reader may be constrained to, the factors motivating him to understand your data, and the information he needs to gather to meet his own goals or make good decisions.

The key questions to ask here are ones like:

- What information does my reader need to be successful?
- How much detail does she need?
- How long does she have to make it effective?

Once you understand the context in which the reader is operating, you can discern which information he needs; and once you understand the filters he may be using, you can discern how best to present that information to him.

Data

The third source of influence in designing a visualization is your data. The best visualizations will reveal what is interesting about the specific data set you're working with. Different data may require different approaches, encodings, or techniques to reveal its interesting aspects. While default visualization formats are a great place to start, and may come with the correct design choices pre-selected, sometimes the data will yield new knowledge when a different visualization approach or format is used.

How do you choose a visualization format that shows your data's best (and most interesting or informative) side? *Know your data*. Respect your data. Instead of shoehorning it into a format that seems slick but doesn't really work, consider the inherent values, relationships, and structures of your data. The type of basic questions you will want to ask about your data include:

- Is it a time-series? A hierarchy?
- How many dimensions does it have? Which are the most important ones?
- What sort of relationships do they have (e.g., one-to-one or many-to-many)?
- How variable are they?

- Are the values categorical? Discrete or continuous? Linear or non-linear? How are they bounded?
- How many categories are there?

If this sounds a little bit like a spec for a database table, it's with good reason. You must understand what you're dealing with in order to treat it well.

This understanding about the shape of your data will inform your design decisions. Each relevant relationship and property of your data needs to be encoded with an appropriate visual property; the characteristics of each dimension of your data will inform which visual property you choose to use to encode it.

Chapter 4, Chapter 5, and Chapter 6 will lead you through some of these questions and decisions more specifically. We will discuss how to make appropriate encoding choices for your data while also taking your reader and your own goals into consideration. But the more you know and understand about each of these sources of influence as you go into the design of your visualization, the better off and more prepared you'll be.

PART II

How Should You Design It?

Now that we know how to think about *why* and *what* we design, both in terms of our purposes and the relationships that define visualizations, let's talk about the *process* of designing visualizations.

Ultimately, the key to a successful visualization is making good design choices. Artists and designers of all kinds study their craft to learn how to do just that. So do programmers. While there is certainly room in these disciplines for creativity (yes, some programming languages are designed to have One Right Way to do things, but most allow for some flexibility and discernment on the part of the programmer), ultimately there is a *process* one follows to determine the optimal outcome for a given project.

Even the most whimsical creators—Jackson Pollock, for instance—use a process. Yes, there is room within that process for playfulness, beauty, and happenstance, but a series of decisions provides a structure that leads from point A to point B. Our aim in this section of the book is to lead you through the process of designing good data visualizations. This should get you 80% of the way to genius; that other 20% is the creative spark you'll have to provide on your own.

In data visualization, the number one rule of thumb to bear is mind is: *Function first, suave second.* Your visualization may look really slick, but if it's not communicating the information you're encoding (and doing so efficiently), then it's just so much visual noise—a pretty picture to put on the wall, maybe, but not a useful tool for imparting information.

Going for sexy, suave, and slick first is an easy trap to fall into. You may begin to notice (with surprise, or not) how very many visualizations, even some by professional designers, fall into this trap. Our goal is to help keep *you* out of it.

But we're using a visual medium, right? So beauty and aesthetics matter?

Absolutely, but there is nothing quite so beautiful as the methodical, streamlined transportation of particulars from one mind to another. This is elegance. This is efficiency. This is your brain on data visualization. And there's a process for that.

Which is, of course, to say that you *can have* suave. You just have to do your due diligence first, so that the visual (or literal!) bells and whistles that you creatively add later on *enhance* and *enable* the function of your design, rather than distract or detract from it.

This part of the book looks at how to do the process properly—from determining your goals, to selecting which dimensions of your data to present and highlight, to planning and implementing a successful encoding—so that you will be successful.

Function first, suave second. Let's go!

CHAPTER 3

Determine Your Goals and Supporting Data

Knowledge Before Structure

OK, here we go, ready to build a visualization! And the first step is...step back and think. Successful products (and software) begin with well-thought-out designs, and spending time thinking before diving into implementation provides a huge return on the time invested up front.

The very first thing to think about is the goal of your visualization. To be useful, that goal must be defined before the implementation phase has started. The visualization (like any product or communication) *must* then be designed with that goal in mind.

The goal of your visualization is going to be informed by your own goals and motivations as well as the needs of your reader. A visualization's goal is usually to satisfy a need for specific information on the part of your reader (an informative visualization, as discussed in Chapter 2). But the goal may also be to change the reader's opinions or behavior in some way (a persuasive visualization, also covered in Chapter 2).

Examples of goals for visualizations include: to monitor systems, find bargains, compare company performances, select suitable solutions, track populations, tell stories, find specific data points, find outliers, show trends, support arguments, or simply give an overview of the data.

 Goals should be stated in terms of the knowledge that can be acquired from the visualization, and should avoid any references to specific content or implementation—don't box yourself into a specific approach yet.

To begin defining the goal of your visualization, ask yourself, *What information need am I attempting to satisfy with this visualization?* Related questions include:

- What values or data dimensions are relevant in this context?
- Which of these dimensions matter; matter most; and matter least?
- What are the key relationships that need to be communicated?
- What properties or values would make some individual data points more interesting than the rest?
- What actions might be taken once this information need is satisfied, and what values will justify that action?

You eventually should be able to *concisely* state the goal of the visualization in *specific terms*, and without motioning any details of implementation. The goal is a pure statement about *function*. Consider which statement in each pair below is the better statement.

- Show the sales figures / Show which product lines are performing best and worst in each region, for each of the last five quarters
- Compare the demographics of Twitter and Facebook users / Compare the ages, education, and income levels of Twitter and Facebook users
- Show a timeline of the performance of every NFL team for the 2011 season / Allow users to compare individual performance metrics for any pair of teams or for the entire league for the 2011 season

While it's obvious that the second statement in each pair is more specific, stop and think for a moment about why they're also better goal statements. They indicate *specific values and relationships* that the visualization should make available to the reader. This level of specificity will directly guide the design process in a particular direction, indicating what data dimensions should be included, how they should be related to each other, *and why*.

In contrast, the first statement of each pair conveys a general intention, but no particular direction, and lends no specific guidance in determining what to include, how it should relate to anything else, or how to tell if and when you've achieved your goals.

 If some statements seem to have conflicts in priority, you may have defined your goals too broadly.

Note also that the better statements have no mention of particular implementations. They don't specify using a timeline or bubble plot or pie graph. They talk about *what* knowledge is displayed, but *not how it is structured*.

As soon as your goal statement includes any detail of implementation, you've killed your own potential for creativity. You have preemptively selected one particular solution out of many that are possible, and constrained all of your future thinking to within the bounds of that box. If you want to be creative and innovative and come up with superior solutions, delay the decisions about implementation as long as possible, until you've really got a good handle on the function you want to provide and the goal you need to achieve. Then you can select (or invent!) the best solution for the parameters of each given situation. The easiest way to think outside the box is to not put your self into a box in the first place.

 Pro tip: this applies to programming (and relationships) as well. For best results, have a complete conversation about desired functionality before you're allowed to discuss implementation.

Having a clear understanding of the goals for your visualization will help you achieve your overall communication goals as well.

Avoiding TMI

Look at your inbox. There are probably too many messages there. A few of them are *really* important. Some are probably somewhat useful. A lot of them are likely noise, and make finding the relevant messages more difficult. The data in a visualization works the same way. The more information that's included, the harder it is to find the information that you (or your readers) care about.

Extraneous content will obscure the message and complicate the extraction of knowledge.

It is tempting to show as much data as possible. We have access to *a lot* of data, and it's easy to be seduced into including more data because it would be cool, or because it's more impressive that way, or simply because we can. But the choice of what to include must be based on the priorities we've discussed: your goals, the needs of your reader, and the shape of your data. It's more powerful to reveal knowledge and facilitate insight than it is to overwhelm with sheer volume.

When reading a visualization (or any other kind of communication), your reader has a limited amount of brainpower to dedicate to the problem (Figure 3-1). Some of this brainpower will be dedicated to *decoding* the visualization; any brainpower that is left may then be used to *understand* the message (if the reader hasn't yet given up in frustration).

In order to be successful, your job is to facilitate understanding by minimizing the amount of extraneous searching and decoding necessary to get the message.

One important way that you can limit the amount of extraneous searching and decoding your reader has to do is to choose encodings that most are easily decoded by the brain. This is the subject of Chapter 4 and Chapter 5, so we will cover it in much more detail shortly.

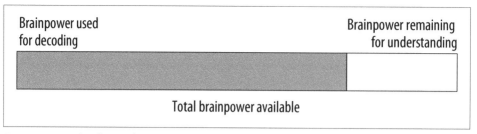

Figure 3-1. Readers have a finite amount of brainpower to apply to your visualization. Any resource used on decoding depletes what is available for understanding.

The other important way that you can limit the amount of extraneous searching and decoding your reader has to do is to be selective about the dimensions of data you choose to encode. Each one should contribute something directly to your message. If you're adding labels or shading, or another full dimension of data, that doesn't contribute to your main message, you're just adding noise. We suggest, instead, embracing a clean, modern aesthetic, and making your important data easier to access.

CHAPTER 4

Choose Appropriate Visual Encodings

Choosing Appropriate Visual Encodings

As we discussed in "Data" on page 16, once you know the "shape" of your data, you can encode its various dimensions with appropriate visual properties. Different visual properties vary—or may be modified—in different ways, which makes them good for encoding different types of data. Two key factors are whether a visual property is *naturally ordered*, and how many *distinct values* of this property the reader can easily differentiate. Natural ordering and number of distinct values will indicate whether a visual property is best suited to one of the main data types: *quantitative*, *ordinal*, *categorical*, or *relational* data. (*Spatial* data is another common data type, and is usually best represented with some kind of map.)

Natural Ordering

Whether a visual property has a natural ordering is determined by whether the mechanics of our visual system and the "software" in our brains automatically—unintentionally—assign an order, or *ranking*, to different values of that property. The "software" that makes these judgments is deeply embedded in our brains and evaluates relative order independent of language, culture, convention, or other learned factors; it's not optional and you can't* design around it.

For example, position has a natural ordering; shape doesn't. Length has a natural ordering; texture doesn't (but pattern density does). Line thickness or weight has a natural ordering; line style (solid, dotted, dashed) doesn't. Depending on the specifics of the visual property, its natural ordering may be well suited to representing *quantitative* differences (27, 33, 41), or *ordinal* differences (small, medium, large, enormous).

Natural orderings are not to be confused with properties for which we have learned or social conventions about their ordering. Social conventions are powerful, and you

---

* Or shouldn't try to: that way madness lies.

should be aware of them, but you *cannot* depend on them to be interpreted in the same way as naturally-ordered properties—which are not social and not learned, and the interpretation of which is not optional.

Color is not ordered

Here's a tricky one: Color (*hue*) is *not* naturally ordered in our brains. Brightness (*lightness* or *luminance*, sometimes called *tint*) and intensity (*saturation*) are, but color itself is not. We have strong social conventions about color, and there is an ordering by wavelength in the physical world, but *color does not have a non-negotiable natural ordering built into the brain.* You can't depend on everyone to agree that yellow follows purple in the way that you can depend on them to agree that four follows three.

The misuse of color to imply order is rampant; don't fall into this common trap. In contexts where you're tempted to use "ordered color" (elevation, heat maps, etc.), consider varying brightness along one, or perhaps two, axes. For example, elevation can be represented by increasing the darkness of browns, rather than cycling through the rainbow (see Figure 4-1[†] and Figure 4-2[‡]).

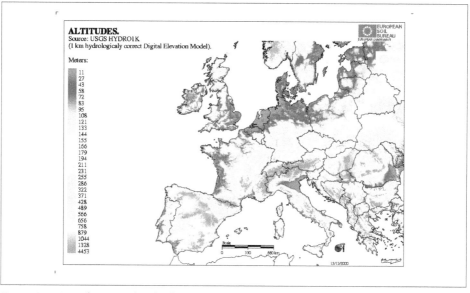

Figure 4-1. A rainbow encoding leads to a map that is very difficult to understand. Does red mean the Alps are hotter than the rest of Europe?

† European Soil Bureau. Copyright © 1995–2011, European Union. Used with stated authorization to reproduce, with acknowledgment. *http://eusoils.jrc.ec.europa.eu/*

‡ Center for International Earth Science Information Network (CIESIN) (2007). Copyright © 2007, The Trustees of Columbia University in the City of New York. Columbia University. Population, Landscape, and Climate Estimates (PLACE). Used under the Creative Commons Attribution License. *http://sedac.ciesin .columbia.edu/place/*

Elevation Zones

Europe

Population, Landscape, and Climate Estimates

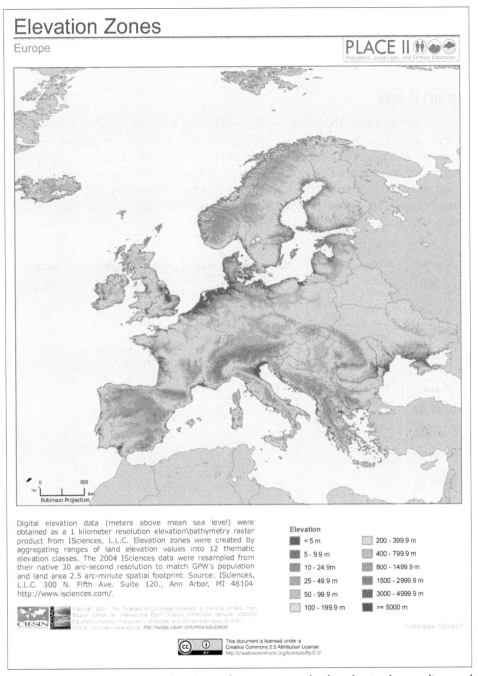

Digital elevation data (meters above mean sea level) were obtained as a 1 kilometer resolution elevation\bathymetry raster product from ISciences, L.L.C. Elevation zones were created by aggregating ranges of land elevation values into 12 thematic elevation classes. The 2004 ISciences data were resampled from their native 30 arc-second resolution to match GPW's population and land area 2.5 arc-minute spatial footprint. Source: ISciences, L.L.C. 300 N. Fifth Ave. Suite 120., Ann Arbor, MI 48104 http://www.isciences.com/.

Elevation

< 5 m		200 - 399.9 m
5 - 9.9 m		400 - 799.9 m
10 - 24.9 m		800 - 1499.9 m
25 - 49.9 m		1500 - 2999.9 m
50 - 99.9 m		3000 - 4999.9 m
100 - 199.9 m		>= 5000 m

Publish Date : 03/13/07

Figure 4-2. In this example the colors diverge from one point, clearly indicating low, medium, and high elevations.

For help in choosing appropriate color palettes, a great tool is Color-Brewer2.0, at *http://colorbrewer2.org*.

Distinct Values

The second main factor to consider when choosing a visual property is how many *distinct values* it has that your reader will be able to perceive, differentiate, and possibly remember. For example, there are a lot of colors in the world, but we can't tell them apart if they're too similar. We can more easily differentiate a large number of shapes, a huge number of positions, and an infinite number of numbers. When choosing a visual property, select one that has a number of useful differentiable values and an ordering similar to that of your data (see Figure 4-3).

Example	Encoding	Ordered	Useful values	Quantitative	Ordinal	Categorical	Relational
	position, placement	yes	infinite	Good	Good	Good	Good
1, 2, 3; A, B, C	text labels	optional alpha or num	infinite	Good	Good	Good	Good
	length	yes	many	Good	Good		
	size, area	yes	many	Good	Good		
	angle	yes	medium	Good	Good		
	pattern density	yes	few	Good	Good		
	weight, boldness	yes	few		Good		
	saturation, brightness	yes	few		Good		
	color	no	few (<20)			Good	
	shape, icon	no	medium			Good	
	pattern texture	no	medium			Good	
	enclosure, connection	no	infinite			Good	Good
	line pattern	no	few				Good
	line endings	no	few				Good
	line weight	yes	few		Good		

Figure 4-3. Use this table of common visual properties to help you select an appropriate encoding for your data type.

Figure 4-4 shows another way to think about visual properties, depending on what kind of data you need to encode. As you can see, many visual properties may be used to encode multiple data types. Position and placement, as well as text, can be used to encode any type of data—which is why every visualization you design needs to begin with careful consideration of how you'll use them (see Chapter 5).

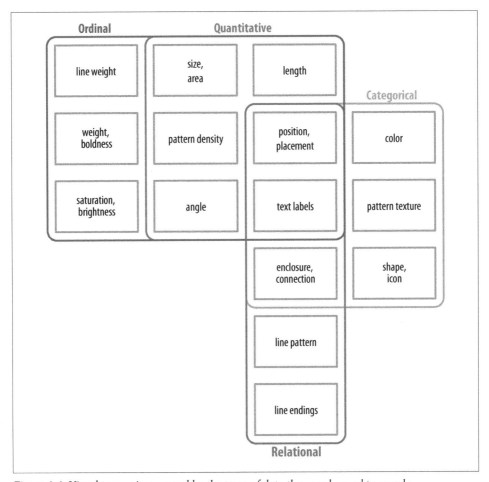

Figure 4-4. Visual properties grouped by the types of data they can be used to encode.

Redundant Encoding

If you have the luxury of leftover, unused visual properties after you've encoded the main dimensions of your data, consider using them to redundantly encode some existing, already-encoded data dimensions. The advantage of *redundant encoding* is that using more channels to get the same information into your brain can make acquisition of that information faster, easier, and more accurate.[§]

For example, if you've got lines differentiated by ending (arrows, dots, etc.), consider also changing the line style (dotted, dashed, etc.) or color. If you've got values encoded by placement, consider redundantly encoding the value with brightness, or grouping regions with color, as in Figure 4-5[II].

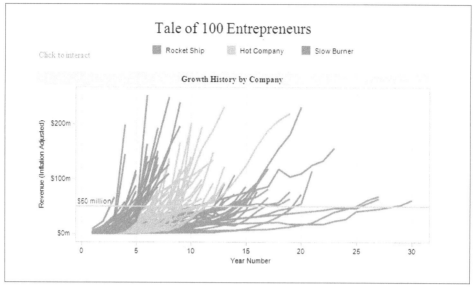

Figure 4-5. Color redundantly encodes the position of groups of companies in this graph.

To be totally accurate, in Figure 4-5, adding color more strongly defined the groupings that weren't strongly defined before, but those groups are a subset of the information already provided by position. For that reason, in this case color adds slightly more informational value beyond mere redundancy.

Defaults versus Innovative Formats

It is worth noting that there are a lot of good *default encodings* and *encoding conventions* in the world, and with good reason. Designing new encoding formats can cost you a lot of time and effort, and may make your reader expend a lot of time and effort to learn. Knowing the expected defaults for your industry, data type, or reader can save you a lot of work when it comes to both figuring out how to best encode your data, and how to explain it to your readers. However, if we all used existing defaults all the time, not much progress would be made. So when should you use a default, and when should you innovate?

§ Ware, *Information Visualization: Perception for Design* (Morgan Kaufmann), p. 179.

‖ Tableau Software Public Gallery. Copyright © 2003–2011 Tableau Software. *http://www.tableausoftware.com/learn/gallery/company-performance*

In writing, we often advise each other to stay away from clichés; don't use a pat phrase, but try to find new ways to say things instead. The reason is that we want the reader to *think* about what we're saying, and clichés tend to make readers turn their brains off. In visualization, however, that kind of brainlessness can be a help instead of a hindrance—since it makes comprehension more efficient—so conventions can be our friends.

 Purposely turning visual convention on its head may cause the reader's brain to "throw an exception," if you will, and this technique can be used strategically; but please, use it sparingly.

The choice comes down to a basic cost-benefit analysis. What is the expense to you and your reader of creating and understanding a new encoding format, versus the value delivered by that format? If you've got a truly superior solution (as evaluated by your reader, and not just your ego), then by all means, use it. But if your job can be done (or done well enough) with a default format, save everyone the effort and use a standard solution.

Readers' Context

In Chapter 2, we discussed how important it is to recognize that you are creating a visualization for someone other than yourself—and that the reader may show up with a mindset or way of viewing the world different from yours.

First, it's important to point out that your audience will likely be composed of *more than one* reader. And as these people are all individuals, they may be as different from each other as they are from you, and will likely have very different backgrounds and levels of interest in your work. It may be impossible to take the preconceptions of all these readers into consideration at once. So choose the most important group, think of them as your *core* group, and design with them in mind. Where it is possible to appeal to more of your potential audience without sacrificing precision or efficiency, do so. But, going forward, let us be clear that when we say *reader*, what we really mean is a representative reader from within your *core audience*.

Okay, now that we've cleared that up, let's get specific about some facets of the reader's mindset that you need to take into account.

Titles, tags, and labels

When selecting the actual terms you'll use to label axes, tag visual elements, or title the piece (which creates the mental framework within which to view it), consider your reader's vocabulary and familiarity with relevant *jargon*.

- Is the reader from within your industry or outside of it? What about other readers outside of the core audience group?

- Is it worth using an industry term for the sake of precision (knowing that the reader may have to look it up), or would a lay term work just as well?
- Will the reader be able to decipher any unknown terms from context, or will a vocabulary gap obscure the meaning of all or part of the information presented?

These are the kinds of questions you should ask yourself. Each and every single word in your visualization needs to serve a specific purpose. For each one, ask yourself: why use this word in this place? Determine whether there is another word that would serve the purpose any better (or whether you can get away without one at all), and if so, make the change.

Related to this, consider any *spelling preferences* a reader might have. Especially within the English language, there may be more than one way to spell a word depending on which country one is in. Don't make the reader's brain do extra work having to parse "superfluous" or "missing" letters.

Colors

Another reader context to take into account is color choice. There is quite a bit of science about how our brains perceive and process color that is somewhat universal, as we saw earlier in this chapter. But it's worth mentioning in the context of reader preconceptions the significant *cultural associations* that color can carry.

Depending on the culture in question, some colors may be lucky, some unlucky; some may carry positive or negative connotations; some may be associated with life events like weddings, funerals, or newborn children.

Some colors don't mean much on their own, but take on meaning when paired or grouped with other colors: in the United States, red and royal blue to Republicans and Democrats; pink and light blue often refer to boys and girls; red, yellow, and green to traffic signals. The colors red, white, and green may signal Christmas in Canada, but patriotism in Italy. The colors red, white, and blue are patriotic in multiple places: they will make both an American and a Frenchman think of home.

Colors may also take on special significance when paired with certain shapes. A red octagon means *stop* in many places (see Figure 4-6#), but not all.

Color blindness

Of course, we know that there are many variations in the way different people perceive color. This is commonly called *color blindness* but is more properly referred to as *color vision deficiency or dyschromatopsia*. A disorder of color vision may present in one of several specific ways.

Christian Caron (2011). Copyright © 2011, Christian Caron.

Figure 4-6. This stop sign from Montreal is labeled in French, but no English speaker is likely to be confused about its meaning.

Although prevalence estimates vary among experts and for different ethnic and national groups, about 7% of American men experience some kind of color perception disorder (women are much more rarely affected: about 0.4 percent in America).* Red-green deficiency is the most common by far, but yellow-blue deficiency also occurs. And there are lots of people who have trouble distinguishing between close colors like blue and purple.

 A great resource for help in choosing color palettes friendly to those with color blindness is the Color Laboratory at *http://colorlab.wickline.org/ colorblind/colorlab/*. There you can select color swatches into a group (or enter custom RGB values) and simulate how they are perceived with eight types of dyschromatopsia. Note: the simulation assumes that you yourself have typical color vision.

Directional orientation

Is the reader from a culture that reads left-to-right, right-to-left, or top-to-bottom? A person's habitual reading patterns will determine their default eye movements over a

---

* Montgomery, Geoffrey, for Howard Hughes Medical Institute. *Seeing, Hearing, and Smelling the World.* Chevy Chase, MD: 1995.

page, and the order in which they will encounter the various visual elements in your design.

It will also affect what the reader perceives as "earlier" and "later" in a timeline, where the edge that is read from will be "earlier" and time will be assumed to progress in the same direction as your reader typically reads text.

This may also pertain to geographic maps: many of us are used to seeing the globe split somewhere along the Pacific, with north oriented upward. This suits North Americans just fine, since—scanning from left to right and starting from the top of the page—we encounter our own country almost immediately. The convention came about thanks to European cartographers, who designed maps over hundreds of years with their own continent as the center of the world.

Occasionally, other map makers have chosen to orient the world map differently, often for the same purpose of displaying their homeland with prominence (such as Stuart McArthur's "South-Up Map," which puts his native Australia toward the center-top) or simply for the purpose of correcting the distortion effect that causes Europe to look bigger than it really is (such as R. Buckminster Fuller's "Dymaxion Map").

Compatibility with Reality

As with so many suggestions in this chapter, a large factor in your success is making life easier for your reader, and that's largely based on making encodings as easy to decode as possible. One way to make decoding easy is to make your encodings of things and relationships as well aligned with the reality (or your reader's reality) of those things and relationships as possible; this alignment is called *compatibility*. This can have many different aspects, including taking cues from the physical world and from cultural conventions.

Things in the world are full of *inherent* properties. These are physical properties that are not (usually) subject to interpretation or culture, but exist as properties you can point to or measure. Some things are larger than others, have specific colors, well-known locations, and other identifying characteristics. If your encodings conflict with or don't reflect these properties, if they are not compatible, you're once again asking your reader to spend extra time decoding and wondering why things are "wrong;" why they don't look like they're expected to (for example, see the boats and airplanes in Figure 4-7).

Figure 4-8 shows an example from *http://html5readiness.com/*.

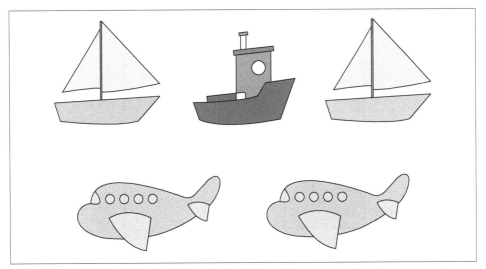

Figure 4-7. The visual placement of boats above airplanes is jarring, since they don't appear that way in the physical world.

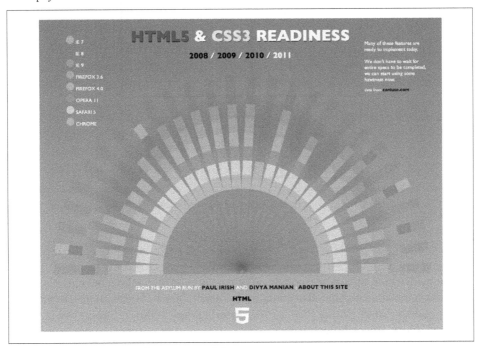

Figure 4-8. Representation of browser capabilities.

Notice how the colors they've chosen map to the browser icons, as shown in Figure 4-9.

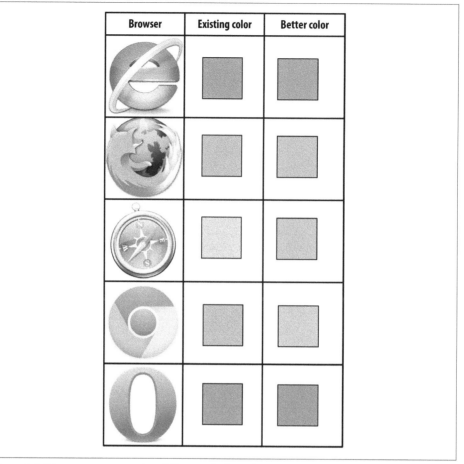

Figure 4-9. The representative colors differ greatly from the colors in the browser icons. Other choices would better reflect the icons' colors.

The encodings they've chosen aren't very compatible with the reality of the browsers' icons and branding. IE, with a blue and yellow icon, is shown in shades of purple. Firefox, with a blue and orange icon, is shown in blue—which is fine, but curious, given the other browser icons that also contain blue and might be better contenders for the blue encoding. Safari, with a blue icon, is encoded with yellow. Chrome—which has red, blue, green, and yellow, but no orange in its icon—is orange. Opera, with its red icon and corresponding red label, has the only encoding that makes sense. An improved set of encodings that more closely match the reality of the browser icons shown in the last column of Figure 4-9.

Beyond physical or *natural* conventions, there are *learned*, cultural conventions that must also be respected. These may not be as easy to point to, but are no less important.

Note that, as we advised in the section on natural ordering, you should not rely on social or cultural conventions to convey information. However, these conventions can be very powerful, and you should be aware that your reader brings them to the table. Making use of them, when possible, to *reinforce* your message will help you convey information efficiently. Avoid countering conventions where possible in order to avoid creating *cognitive dissonance*, a clash of habitual interpretation with the underlying message you are sending.

To use colors as an example of some of these learned conventions, red and green have strong connotations for bad and good, or stop and go. (See the Color section in Chapter 6 for more on common color associations.) Beyond color, consider cultural conventions about spatial representations, such as what left and right mean politically, or the significance of above and below. Also consider cultural conventions about the meaning or square versus round, and bright versus dark.

All sorts of metaphorical interpretations are culturally ingrained. An astute designer will think about these possible interpretations and work with them, rather than against them.

Direction and reality

Direction is an interesting property to consider because it has both inherent and learned conventions. How many times have you looked at an emergency exit map in a hallway, and realized that the exit, displayed to the left on the map, was to your right in reality, because the map was upside down relative to the direction you were facing?[†] You may also run into maps that, for various reasons, don't put north at the top of the map. Even though the map may be fully accurate and not violating compatibility with physical reality, this violation of cultural convention can be enormously disorienting.

Patterns and Consistency

The human brain is *amazingly* good at identifying patterns in the world. We easily recognize similarity in shapes, position, sound, color, rhythm, language, behavior, and physical routine, just to name a few variables. This ability to recognize patterns is extremely powerful, as it enables us to *identify stimuli* that we've encountered before, and *predict behavior* based on what happened the last time we encountered a similar stimulus pattern. This is the foundation of language, communication, and all learning. The ability to recognize patterns and learn from them allows us to notice and respond when we hear the sound of our name, to run down a set of stairs without hurting ourselves, and to salivate when we smell food cooking.

Consequently, we also notice *violations of patterns*. When a picture is crooked, a friend sounds troubled, a car is parked too far out into the street, or the mayonnaise smells

---

† Your authors take particular interest in examining information design in the world, take every opportunity to do so, and hope that everyone else will start to do the same.

wrong, the patterns we expect are being violated and *we can't help but notice* these exceptions. Flashing lights and safety vests are intentionally designed to stand out from the background—we notice them because they are exceptions to the norm.

Practically speaking, this pattern and pattern-violation recognition has two major implications for design. The first is that *readers will notice patterns* and assume they are intentional, whether you planned for the patterns to exist or not. The second is that when they perceive patterns, *readers will also expect pattern violations to be meaningful.*

As designers, we must be extremely deliberate about the patterns and pattern violations we create. Don't arbitrarily assign positions or colors or connections or fonts with no rhyme or reason to your choices, because your reader will always assume that you meant something by it. If you change the order or membership of a list of items, either in text or in placement, it will be perceived as meaningful. If you change the encoding of items, by position, shape, color, or other methods, it will be perceived as meaningful.

So how should you avoid the potential trap of implying meaning where none is intended? It all comes down to three simple rules.

- Be consistent in membership, ordering, and other encodings.
- Things that are the same should look the same.
- Things that are different should look different.

These sound simple, and yet violations of these rules are everywhere. You can probably think of a few already, and will probably start to notice more examples in your daily life. Maintaining consistency and intention when encoding will greatly enhance the accessibility and efficiency of your visualization, and, as with any good habit, will make your life easier in the long run.

Selecting Structure

Just as we don't write PhD dissertations in sonnet form, or thank-you notes like legal briefs complete with footnote citations, it's important that the structure of your visualization be appropriate to your data.

The structure of a visualization should *reveal* something about the underlying data. Take, for example, one of the most classic data visualizations: the Periodic Table of the Elements (Figure 4-10‡). This is arguably one of the most elegant visualizations ever made. It takes a complex dataset and makes it simple, organized, and transparent. The elements are laid out in order by atomic number, and by wrapping the rows at strategic points, the table reveals that elements in various categories occur at regular intervals, or *periods*. The table makes it easier to understand the nature of each element—both individually, and in relation to the other elements we know of.

---

‡ Michael Dayah (1997). Copyright © 1997 Michael Dayah. *http://www.ptable.com*

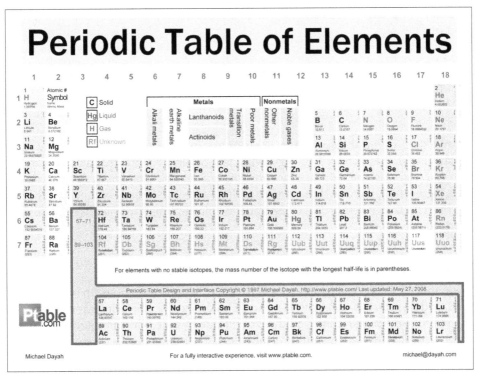

Figure 4-10. *This rendition of the classic table makes good use of color and line.*

Perhaps because it is so elegant and iconic, the Periodic Table is also one of the most frequently imitated visualizations out there. Designers and satirists are constantly re-purposing its familiar rows and columns to showcase collections of everything from typefaces to video game controllers, and, ironically, visualization methods. This phenomenon is a particular peeve to your authors precisely because it violates the important principle of selecting an appropriate structure. With the possible (yet questionable) exception of Andrew Plotkin's Periodic Table of Desserts,[§] copycat designers are using a periodic structure to display data that is *not periodic*. They are just so many derivative attempts at cleverness.

If you're using a particular structure just to be cute or clever, you're doing it wrong.

If you are tempted to use a periodic table format for your non-periodic data, consider instead a two-axis scatter plot or table, where the axes are well matched to the important

[§] *http://eblong.com/zarf/periodic/index.html*

aspects of your data. This will lead you to a more accurate, and less derivative, final product.[||]

 For another chemistry-oriented example of a specific structure with an entirely different purpose, check out the Table of Nuclides: *http://en .wikipedia.org/wiki/Table_of_nuclides*

Beyond that, we must refer you to other tomes (we suggest the books by Yau and Kosslyn listed in Appendix A to begin with, and Bertin for more dedicated readers) to help you select just the right structure for your particular circumstance; as you can see from Figure 4-11, there are too many to address each one directly within the scope of this short book. But here are some general principles and common pitfalls to guide your selection process.C

Comparisons Need to Compare

If you intend to allow comparison of values, set the representations up in equivalent ways, and then *put them close together*. You wouldn't ask people to look at two versions of a photo in different rooms; you'd put them side-by-side. The same goes for visualizations, particularly with quantitative measures. If you want people to be able to meaningfully compare values, put them as near to each other as possible.

Another important comparison principle is that of *preservation*. Just as you would isolate variables in a clinical trial by comparing a test group to a control group—which is similar to the test group except for one variable—you need to isolate visual changes by preserving other conditions, so that the change may be easily and fairly interpreted.

A good example of this is in comparing two graphs. Beware of what scales you use on your axes so that the reader can fairly interpret the graph data. If one graph has a scale of 0 to 10 and the other has a scale of 0 to 5 (Figure 4-11), the slopes displayed on the graphs will be very different for the same data. Using unequal scales for data you are attempting to compare makes comparison much more difficult.

Some Structures Are Just Inherently Bad

Some formats are just *bad*, and should never be used under any circumstances. Many of the formats that fall into this category do so because they *distort proportion*. There are certain things that our brains are and aren't good at: for example, we are terrible at comparing lengths of curved lines and the surface areas of irregularly-shaped fields. For this reason, concentric circle graphs (see, for example, *http://michaelvandaniker.com/*

[||] Astute readers will note that the periodic table is also a two-axis layout with carefully chosen axes that reflect, and facilitate access to, the relevant properties of the data.

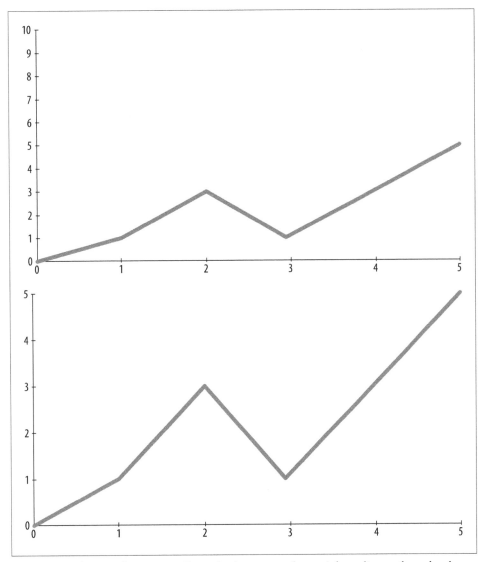

Figure 4-11. The same data appears flatter (top) or steeper (bottom) depending on the scales chosen. If we were attempting to compare these data sets, the unequal axes would introduce distortion that made comparison more difficult.

blog/2009/10/31/visualizing-historic-browser-statistics-with-axiis/) are one of the worst offenders in the world of data presentation structures.#

#We care so much about this issue that we dedicate a section in Chapter 5 to good and bad uses of circular layouts.

If I show you a section of the ring in the middle that represents a huge percentage, it still looks objectively shorter than a section of the outer ring that may represent a much smaller percentage. Also, having all of these lines wrapped in a circle makes it difficult to compare their lengths anyway. They only way you can really grasp the information represented in this graph is to read the percentage numbers in the labels. In this case, we may as well just have a table of numbers—it would be faster to read and easier to make comparisons with.

Similarly, the ringed pie graph format known as Nightingale's Rose (for its creator, Florence—see Figure 4-12), is almost completely useless. Comparing the areas of the sliced pie wedges is nearly impossible to do accurately. Line graphs or stacked bar graphs would have served much better.

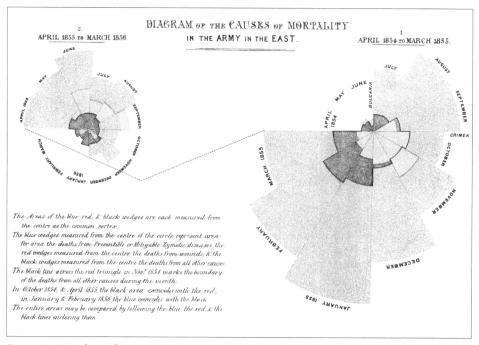

Figure 4-12. Nightingale's Rose.

Unfortunately, this format continues to be reinvented in all sorts of modern contexts. See Figure 4-13 for an equally useless implementation using the same variously sized pie wedges.

Some Good Structures Are Often Abused

There are bad formats, and then there are good formats frequently misused. Like the Periodic Table, pie graphs are useful for a very specific purpose, but quickly devolve into unhelpful parody when drafted into extended service.

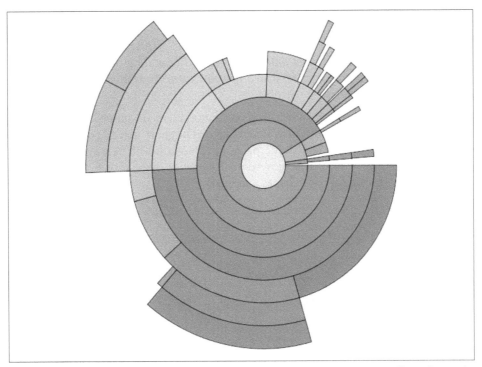

Figure 4-13. A radial layout distorts the data and renders this disk usage map totally ineffective for all but the coarsest comparisons.

The specialty of a pie graph is comparison—specifically, comparison of a few parts to a larger whole. We've already established above in our discussion of concentric circle graphs and Nightingale's Roses that the human brain is lousy at comparing the lengths and surface areas of curved or irregularly-shaped fields; pie graphs fall directly into this category.

Another common pitfall is the use of a geographic map for any and all data that includes a location dimension. Sometimes the use of a map will actually distort your message— such as when the surface area of each region fails to correspond to your population data (see the section on physical reality in Chapter 5). If your data is tied to population but your display is based on regional size, the proportionally larger surface areas of some regions may inflate the appearance of trends in those regions. Consider using a table or bar graph instead.

 If you wish to show regional trends, remember that you don't have to position states or countries alphabetically; it's okay to group them by region or along some other appropriate axis.

Keep It Simple (or You Might Look) Stupid

We talked about careful selection of visual content in Chapter 3, and will talk about selecting and applying encodings well in Chapter 6. But editing (in the sense of minimizing noise to maximize signal) is also a key concept to bear in mind for selecting a useful structure (and *keeping* it useful).

Consider Figure 4-14, which shows an organization chart developed in 2010 by the Joint Economic Committee minority, Republicans. The chart, titled "Your New Health Care System," depicts the Democratic party's proposed health care system, and displays a bewildering array of new government agencies, regulations, and mandates, represented by a tangled web of shapes and lines.

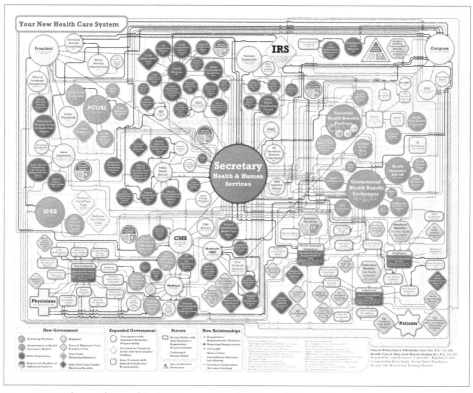

Figure 4-14. This rendition of the healthcare plan clearly revels in and aims to exaggerate the system's complexity.

It's fairly obvious that political motivations dominated the design choices for this visualization; it clearly falls into the category of persuasive visualization (rather than informative). The chart itself doesn't leave the reader with any actual information other than, "Wow, this system is complicated." When we consider the title of the press release in which this was unveiled—"America's New Health Care System Revealed"—we know those responsible to be disingenuous.

A citizen designer, Robert Palmer, took it upon himself to make a different, cleaner visual representation of the same proposed health care plan (Figure 4-15*). His chart is strikingly different from the one created by the Joint Economic Committee minority.

Palmer explained his motivation in an open letter to Rep. John Boehner (R-OH) on Flickr (*http://www.flickr.com/photos/robertpalmer/3743826461/*) (*http://www.flickr .com/photos/robertpalmer/3743826461/*):

> By releasing your chart, instead of meaningfully educating the public, you willfully obfuscated an already complicated proposal. There is no simple proposal to solve this problem. You instead chose to shout "12! 16! 37! 9! 24!" while we were trying to count something.[†]

There is no doubt that national healthcare is a complex matter, and this is evident in both designs. But Palmer's rendition clearly aims to pare down that complexity to its essential nature, for the purpose of making things *easier to understand*, rather than purposefully clouding what is happening under the abstracted layer. This is the hallmark of effective editing.

Sometimes a designer will make the visualization more complicated than it need to be, not because he is trying to make the data look bad, but for precisely the opposite reason: he wants the data to look as good as possible. This is an equally bad mistake.

Your data is important and meaningful all on its own; you don't have to make it special by trying to get fancy. Every dot, line and word should serve a communicative purpose: if it is extraneous or outside the scope of the visualization's goals, it must go. *Edit ruthlessly*. Don't decorate your data.

---

* Robert Palmer (2010). Copyright © 2010, Robert Palmer. *http://rp-network.com/*

† *http://www.flickr.com/photos/robertpalmer/3743826461/*

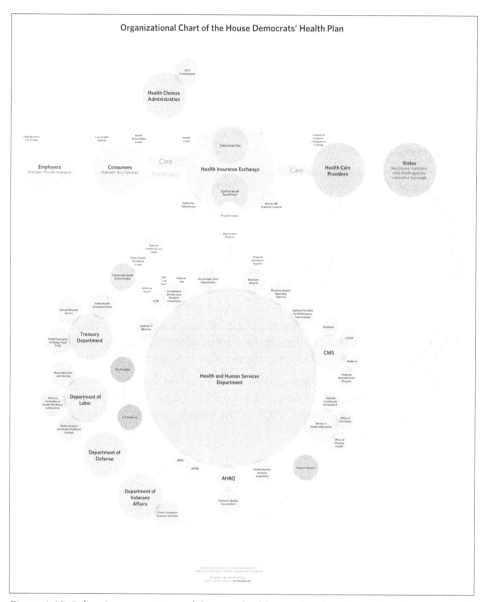

Figure 4-15. Palmer's representation of the same healthcare plan doesn't oversimplify, but is much easier to parse.

CHAPTER 5

First, Place

Now that you have had a chance to define your goals, identify some supporting data, and consider appropriate visual encodings, it's time to think about he particulars of how to apply those encodings. That means making some decisions about what placement will signify and where particular visual entities will go on the page, what attributes (such as color, size, and texture) you will assign them, and how you will label and describe them.

If you haven't already done so, now would be an excellent time to get out some paper and pens, open a sketching application on your computer, or avail yourself of whatever prototyping method most suits you. Ideally, it will be something quick and dirty and malleable (so you can try out lots of options), with various color and typographic choices available.

We'll start with a discussion of *spatial position*—axes and placement—because this property defines the scope and visual landscape that your visualization will occupy. For this and other reasons, spatial position is often the most important visual encoding you'll have to select. Once we have covered basic placement and organization, we'll move on to color and other visual encoding properties in Chapter 6.

Position: Layout and Axes

Axes (and the resulting layout), placement, and position of entities are perhaps the most underutilized visual encodings. While axes are frequently defined, they are often not used to their fullest potential, or not assigned at all. When this happens, opportunities to communicate information are lost or wasted, efficiency suffers, understanding becomes more difficult, and your reader cries. No one wants that, and the problem is largely avoidable with a bit of consideration.

Position Is Your Most Powerful Encoding

As discussed in Chapter 4, *physical position is the easiest to perceive and most powerful visual property,*[*] but this power is only accessible if you chose to use it. It's not difficult to use, and—when used properly—it can convey a huge amount of information. Position can encode as many discrete values as you have room to display (sometimes more), and can indicate ordered, temporal, categorical, quantitative, or quantitative values, as well as causal, correlative, sequential, qualitative, or quantitative relationships.

Any values in any data dimension that can be expressed or described as "these values are different than those values" can be encoded with position, if you use a correspondingly defined axis.

Axes contribute value in two ways: both from the bottom up and from the top down. From the bottom up, an entity inherits values from an axis or axes without requiring the use of any extra ink or labeling on that entity. The reader can easily look at *where* the entity is placed *relative to an axis or axes* and understand that the values that correspond to that position on the axis apply to the entity in question. The entity doesn't need to be labeled "first" or "Western" or "less valuable"; those values are (appropriately) implied by position alone when an axis is defined.

Conversely, if the reader is looking for entities with a specific value or range of values, well-defined axes can help limit the scope of their search to the groups or subsets of entities that have that value. This is the top-down approach. If you're looking for desserts on a menu,[†] you only need to look in the desserts section. If you're looking for the most recent events in a timeline, you can look exclusively at the most recent end of the time axis. If you're looking for restaurants near your location on a map, you can easily just look at restaurants that have location values near your own.

The entities found using these search methods don't need to be labeled with those specific values; it's understood that they inherit those values from the axes. And entities outside of your defined search range can safely be ignored: examination and evaluation of each out-of-range entity is not necessary, because placement alone tells us they're irrelevant.

Consider the periodic table once again. It's clear that the periods and groups, encoded in the rows and columns, are the defining characteristic of the table. Well-defined axes and the corresponding placement of each element are responsible for making the periodic table the valuable tool that it is. The axes allow readers to find (and predict the

---

[*] Jock Mackinlay 1986, reprinted in Card, Mackinlay, and Shneiderman. *Readings in Information Visualization: Using Vision to Think*. Morgan Kauffman, 1999: pg 73. Originally from Cleveland and McGill, "Graphical Perception: Theory, Experimentation, and Application to the Development of Graphical Methods." *Journal of the American Statistical Association*. Vol. 79, No. 387, Sept., 1984. *http://www.jstor.org/stable/2288400*.

[†] Most print menus have one linear, categorical axis that roughly correlates to order-of-eating—for example, labeled: appetizers, soups and salads, main plates, and desserts.

existence of) elements of interest, and understand relevant properties of each element based purely on its position in the table.

Consider placement first

While position isn't the best possible encoding method for all data dimensions in all situations, its power and broad applicability mean you should deeply consider how best to use position. It should be one of, if not *the*, first encoding you define for your visualization. It should be considered for your most important values and relationships (and at this point you should have determined what those are).

What's the most common error we observe with axes and placement? Not using them. Tragically often, visualizations don't have any axes defined, or only define a single axis.

 Consider the following challenge. For every visualization you see, ask yourself these two questions: Are the axes all well defined? Are they used effectively? Unfortunately, the answer to these is often "no." Better use of axes will be the first step to improvement.

While there are situations where two good axes aren't obvious—or use of a second axis doesn't make sense—it's always worth considering how a second axis could convey meaning. Got a timeline? Consider a data dimension that could benefit from ordering the other axis. Arranging by rank? Think about what other properties your entities could be sorted or grouped by. Are you clumping or clustering entities based on their relationship to each other (as in social network diagrams)? Consider how clumps relate to each other, or which entities or relationships have ordered values.

Try using position for different data dimensions. Swap your axes. Play with them. Interrogate your assumptions. Iterate. The following sections will give you some ideas to consider when thinking about placement.

The Meaning of Placement and Proximity

Let's take a moment to consider how your various visually encoded entities should be placed on the page. Here are some principles to bear in mind.

Semantic Distance and Relative Proximity

There's a literary term used to describe the conceptual relatedness of objects or ideas: *semantic distance*. A housecat, for instance, is semantically closer to a tiger than to a water buffalo. But it may be closer to a water buffalo than to an orchid, or to Neuschwanstein Castle. Thus we can see that with semantic difference, not only does proximity matter, but *relative proximity* matters.

The same is true of visual proximity on a page (or screen). Entities that are closer to one another on paper will be perceived as *conceptually closer* than entities located further away from each other. And an entity will be perceived as *relatively* more conceptually related to whatever entity is closest to it. The reader's brain will then "create" a category to explain the apparent groups; switching two of the entities will cause the reader to "see" a different category (see Figure 5-1 and Figure 5-2‡).

Figure 5-1. Placing the housecat closer to the tiger shows that it is semantically closer to that than to the other items, and forms the category felines.

Absolute Placement

Absolute placement on the page or screen also carries meaning. All else being equal, elements toward the top of the page are generally considered more important than elements on the bottom. Most people also read from the top down, so items at the top will be read first (and if the content isn't compelling enough, the reader may never make it to the bottom).

Representation of Physical Space

When no other compelling and meaningful ordering exists, consider placing items on the page (or screen) in the same relative order as they'd be found in the physical world.

---

‡ Figure 5-1 and Figure 5-2 photo credits to: Annette Crimmins, Sias van Schalkwyk, Janni Due, Dimitri Castrique, and Grethe Boe.

Figure 5-2. Putting the water buffalo closer to the tiger causes your brain to think of a new category: perhaps, safari animals.

Also, when possible, be aware of your reader's orientation in physical space, and arrange the visual elements accordingly. We've all read maps at the mall or in other large public spaces that tell you, "You Are Here." Often, those maps fail to correspond to the reality of the physical space; things on the left of the map aren't actually to the reader's left, etc. You may not always know where your reader will be standing or how they will be oriented, but make your best guess whenever possible.

 Consider letting the reader's probable orientation in physical space trump other considerations and conventions (such as putting due North at the top of the page).

Logical Relationships versus Physical Relationships

Though we've talked about how representation and encoding should match reality as closely as possible, to aid the reader's intuitive understanding, there are situations for which this isn't true. Sometimes the relationships that need to be communicated are more important than the physical (or understood) relative positions. When selecting your layout, consider which of these is the more important consideration.

Patterns and Grouped Objects

One of the cool things our brains are really good at is automatically collecting and grouping disparate elements into a cohesive set. For this reason, you don't look at a zebra and perceive, for instance, 43 vertical lines of about one arm's length each, at varying positions—you just see "stripes." Our brains automatically group and assimilate similar features in proximity to each other. This is another way to say that our brains are great at picking up on *patterns*.§

It's important to be aware of this function of the visual system, because it may come into play unexpectedly, causing your reader's brain to group or otherwise relate proximate elements within your visualization into a pattern you didn't intend, or to perceive as a unified object some disparate elements you meant to remain individual.

 It may be difficult for you to anticipate these unintended perceptions in the same way that it's sometimes difficult to catch typos in your own writing: your brain already knows what you meant. Try asking a friend or coworker to take a look at your mock-ups periodically to give you feedback until you've learned what kinds of groupings to avoid.

On the other hand, taking advantage of this grouping habit can be a great way to intentionally convey affinity or similarity without using any other labels or ink.

Patterns of Organization (and More!)

In *Information Anxiety* (Doubleday), Richard Saul Wurman proposed that there are just five ways to organize information, and suggested the mnemonic acronym LATCH:

- Location
- Alphabetical
- Time
- Categorical
- Hierarchical

While it could be argued that *alphabetical* and *time* are subsets of his broad *hierarchy* category (which encompasses any ordered or ranked information), we find it remains a useful list to consider.‖ Within or beyond that list, consider the following sorts of relationships as possible axes or positional organizational schemes.

---

§ For more discussion of the shortcuts our brains take, read about the behaviors described by Gestalt psychology: *http://en.wikipedia.org/wiki/Gestalt_psychology#Pr.C3.A4gnanz*.

‖ Note the similarity to the list of data types at the beginning of Chapter 4.

In most cases, when organizing your data, you should place the most important (or first) piece of information at the left end or top, and the least important, or last, at the right end or bottom.

Importance
A hierarchy variant where the most relevant information or the most important entities are at one end (usually the top or left) and the least important are at the opposite end. This works for everything from organizational charts to sales figures. Importance can also apply to your own priority and the direction you want the reader to consume the information.

Causality
Cause and effect, whether linear or cyclical, is a powerful organizational structure. If the organization is cyclical, consider a round structure, probably moving clockwise. Otherwise, causality probably flows from cause on the left to effect on the right (unless your local language reads right to left).

Dependence
This is a great organizational scheme in which entities can be ranked as relatively more dependent and independent. Consider this for hierarchically related entities, such as object classes, libraries, etc.

Categorical
Not hierarchical, but absolutely useful. Consider clumping or grouping otherwise-unordered data into categories. If nothing else, it'll help your reader make sense of the volume of data you're presenting.

Specific Graphs, Layouts, and Axis Styles

Here is a list of some common visualization layouts and formats. For an incredibly exhaustive reference to graph and diagram styles, see *Information Graphics* (Oxford University Press), by Robert Harris.

Quantitative and comparative formats

Bar graphs
This is one of the most common and most useful graph types. Bar graphs are your go-to graph for *comparing data values* within or across categories. Bar graphs are good for *discrete data*; for continuous data, consider using a line graph.

To be precise, the bars on a bar graph are horizontal; graphs with vertical bars are *column graphs*. But everyone calls them *bar graphs* anyway.

Bars can contain multiple, stacked data values within the category. Stacking values can make comparing the upper values difficult, because they don't share a common baseline with the same data dimension in other bars. For this reason, carefully consider which values you put at the bottom of each bar. We suggest the most relevant or important data dimension. (And of course, stack all of your bars in the same order!)

Histograms

Histograms are specialized bar graphs designed to *show distribution of values across a possible range*. The total area of the graph represents the sum total of all of the values present. The granularity of the categories on the horizontal axis can be as coarse or narrow as is useful.

Line graphs

Line graphs are your workhorse for *continuous data*. Line graphs are great for showing trends, and—for the right kind of data—can be far less cluttered than bar graphs. Typically, line graphs have the independent data dimension progressing along the horizontal axis, and the dependent data dimension along the vertical axis. However, there are cases where the data isn't related in such a way.

When designing filled-area line graphs, be very clear to indicate whether the graph values accumulate vertically, or whether they are layered in front of one another, as shown in Figure 5-3.

The best practice is to use filled area only when you intend for the values to accumulate vertically, and to use simple lines when the values are not accumulating.

Time series

Data with a time dimension probably should be displayed on a time series graph, with time values typically progressing left to right on the horizontal axis, and another data dimension displayed on the vertical axis. Time series data that is qualitative may be better represented with a timeline, where the horizontal axis is still time, but the vertical axis may be qualitative or categorical.

Pie graphs

Pie graphs are valid for *comparing fractions of a whole*. Best used when there are few relevant fractions, and precision isn't required. For more detail on valid uses, see "Pie graphs" under "Good uses of circles and circular layouts" on page 58. As an alternative, consider stacked bar graphs.

Scatter plots

Scatter plots are great for looking for *correlations between two quantitative dimensions of data*, or for displaying *data that varies along two dimensions*. Three and four dimensions are possible by encoding data points as bubbles, pies, or stacked bar graphs.

Tables

Tables of text values, while not a visualization in the sense that we usually think of, are the display method of choice when *data precision* is required. Tables can be

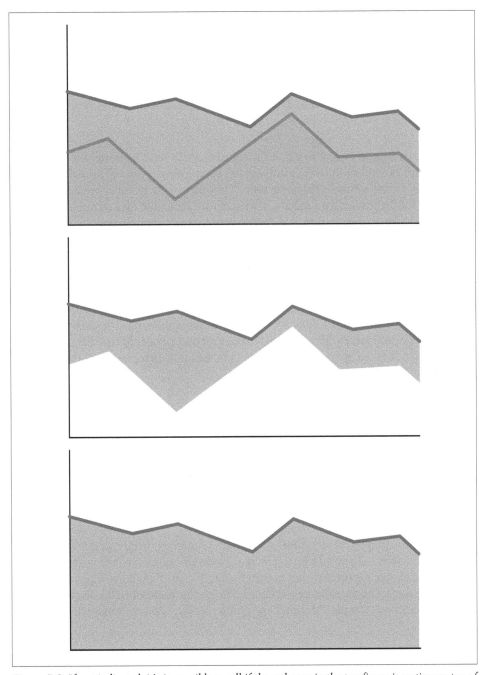

Figure 5-3. If not indicated, it's impossible to tell if the red area in the top figure is resting on top of the blue area and only represents the area shown in the middle figure, or if it's behind the blue, and occupies the full height down to the horizontal axis, as shown in the bottom figure.

an effective compliment for visualization styles where trends are visible, but precision is harder to perceive. Note that table cells can contain data other than text, and the cell itself can be encoded with color or other visual properties, as in the Periodic Table of the Elements.

Periodic tables

Best choice for *periodic data*. There are *no* other rigorously valid use cases. None. Not even if it's *really* clever.

Treemaps

Treemaps (not to be confused with tree diagrams) were invented by Ben Shneiderman# as a solution to the problem of representing *proportional values and hierarchal relationships at the same time*. They are excellent for representing many hierarchically nested data values. Treemaps are typically used to represent distribution and use of resources, such as budgets or computer storage.

Heat maps

Heat maps are two-dimensional area graphs that use color or brightness to indicate *values (or changes in value) of large data sets*. Color can be used to indicate areas of large changes, out-of-range values, or other interesting characteristics. While red-green or red-yellow-green color schemes are common, best practices include muting unremarkable values so that interesting values have a greater contrast against normal values. This can also make heat maps easier to read for people with color blindness. In some instances, it can be easier to perceive small-multiple line graphs than colored sections.*

Small multiples

Small multiples are arrays of very small, not very detailed graphs that allow the reader to *compare the sense or trend of many values concurrently*, or to show how a set of values changes over time. Small multiples are often line graphs, but can be made of other appropriate graph styles. Often, small multiples are used in the way heat maps are, as a quick dashboard or interface that allows the reader to identify interesting values for further investigation. Though not invented by him, small multiples have been popularized and advocated for by Edward Tufte.

Marimekko (also known as matrix or mosaic) graphs

Marimekko graphs are bar graphs with bars of uniform height that are stacked in two directions to form a larger rectangle. The width of each column varies, so that its surface area represents that column's fraction of the whole. The sum of each column's stacked sections represents 100% of the value of that column. There's an interactive sample Marimekko graph at *http://www.freakalytics.com/marimekko*.

#See *http://www.cs.umd.edu/hcil/treemap-history/index.shtml.*

* See *http://people.seas.harvard.edu/~miriah/pathline.org/pathline.pdf.*

Relational formats

Data flow diagrams, Entity Relationship Diagrams, etc.
   There are a large number of relational technical formats used to document the flow of data through a process, the flow of a user through a software interface or website, the relationship among classes or database tables, etc. These all can benefit from an organized layout, sorted by level of abstraction, chronology, importance, hierarchy, or other relevant classification.

Decision maps and flow charts
   These relational diagrams track the path of a process or decision. Nodes represent choices, actions, or other tests or states (see Figure 5-X). Node type is usually encoded with shape, and often with color as well. UML behavior diagrams[†] are examples of this type of visualization.

Social network graphs
   A version of node-edge (or box-and-arrow) graphs, used to display connections among people, companies, etc. At the most basic level, they represent one kind of node (such as "person") and one kind of relationship (such as "acquainted"). More interesting social network graphs may include different kinds of nodes and different kinds of relationships or connections. Genograms (family trees) are a specific kind of social network graph.

Spatial formats

Geographic map
   The topic of mapping is far too vast to be thoroughly addressed here. We will say that some common practices for representing data on maps include color coding geographic regions; overlaying lines to represent relationships, connections, or movements of things or data; and representing local quantities with bubbles or pies per region. Another approach involves distorting the representation of physical space to reflect logical meaning in the data; the resulting map is called a *cartogram*.

Non-geographic map
   Images can use the metaphorical idea of spatial relations to represent any number of other concepts, from mapping a winning strategy to product maps, to the map of my heart. Leveraging a spatial metaphor can be a powerful way to convey intent, relationship, sequence, influence, and process. As you might suspect, the key to success in these constructed contexts is to define (and communicate) the parameters of the space in such a way that your reader understands what placement and direction mean in your map.

† *http://en.wikipedia.org/wiki/Unified_Modeling_Language#Diagrams_overview.*

Appropriate Use of Circles and Circular Layouts

Circles are really pretty. Round, natural—maybe even sensual. They're also very frequently used to represent data. And sadly, for all of their beauty, circles and circular layouts are usually used improperly, in ways that don't allow efficient decoding of the data.

The fundamental problem with using circles is that we're not very good at estimating and comparing circular areas and radial measures, such as arc lengths and pie wedge sizes. Comparisons of rectangular length and area are much easier to understand. With that in mind, we present a short list of appropriate and inappropriate uses for circles and circular layouts.

Good uses of circles and circular layouts

Cyclical relationships

> Annual seasons, 24-hour days, biological processes such as the Krebs Cycle, or any other repeating phenomenon can be well-represented by a circular layout. These are successful uses because reality actually involves a cyclical relationship wherein the last phase of one cycle leads clearly into the first phase of the next cycle (see Figure 5-4).
>
> Please be careful not to use circular layouts to represent "cycles" for which the process may repeat, but the starting phase doesn't (or shouldn't) follow from the previous ending phase. This is capably demonstrated by the Federal Emergency Management Agency in Figure 5-5.

Direction

> When dealing with directional data, round layouts that represent direction are entirely appropriate and useful, as they directly indicate the physical reality of direction. The wind roses in Figure 5-6[‡] show wind frequency and speed by direction. This presentation is more easily understandable than a bar graph or table of data.

Pie graphs

> Few formats evoke as strong a response on the part of data visualization professionals as pie graphs.[§] Some experts say, "Never, ever, ever use pie graphs!" Others say, "Just watch kids argue at a pizza party and it's clear that people can judge angles!" The truth lies somewhere in between.
>
> We *can* estimate round surface area, and we can estimate relative angle sizes (and hence, compare pie-wedge areas). However, there are a few relevant caveats.
>
> - We're better at comparing rectangular areas than circular areas, so comparison of bar length is easier than comparison of circle sizes.

[‡] Nelson Minar (2011). Copyright © 2011 Daedalus Bits, LLC. *http://windhistory.com/*

[§] Pedantic clarification: graphs deal with quantitative data, charts, such as org charts and flow charts, with qualitative or relational data. Therefore, "pie charts" are properly called *pie graphs*.

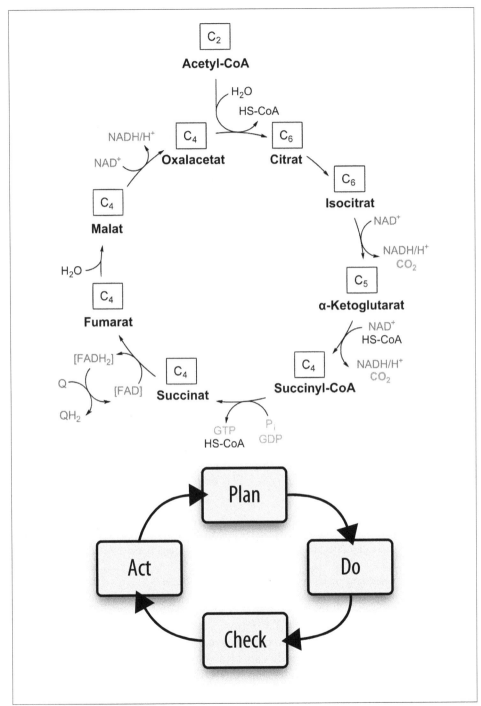

Figure 5-4. Good use of circular layout: Krebs Cycle (top) and Deming Cycle (bottom).

Figure 5-5. FEMA misunderstands cyclical causality.

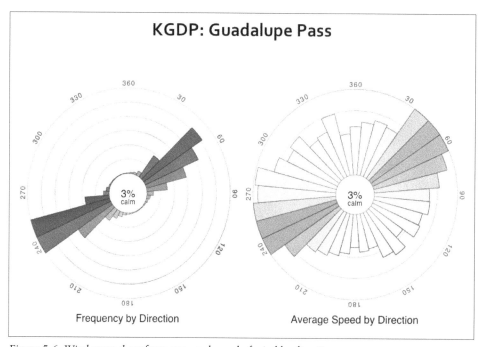

Figure 5-6. Wind roses show frequency and speed of wind by direction.

- We're better at comparing length than angles, so comparison of bar length is easer than comparison of pie wedges.
- We're better at comparing shapes that have a common baseline than shapes that don't, so comparing wedges that are rotated relative to each other is more challenging than comparing angles that start at the same place.

The bottom line is that pie graphs are best used when precision isn't particularly important, and when there are relatively few wedges to compare (or few that matter). See Figure 5-7[||].

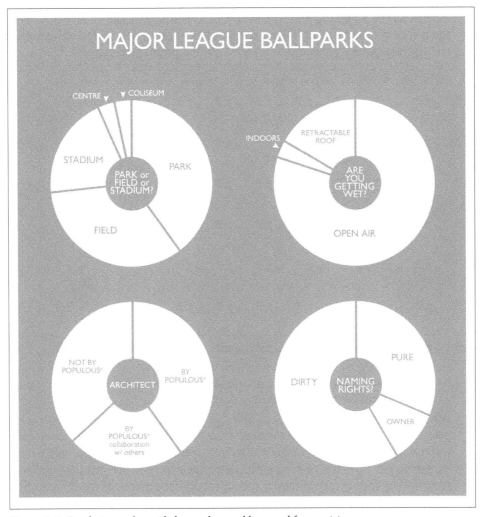

Figure 5-7. Good pie graphs, with few wedges and low need for precision.

While there are some valid uses of pie graphs, in most cases, there's a rectangular solution that is as good or better. For comparing fractions of a whole, stacked bar graphs are the most common alternative. For comparing fractions to each other,

|| Craig Robinson (2011). Copyright © 2011, Craig Robinson. *http://www.flipflopflyin.com/flipflopflyball/info-majorleagueparks.html*

standard bar graphs are preferred. That's not to say, "Never use pie graphs"—just use them selectively.

Area on bubble graphs

Circles are often well used as a third quantitative measure when two other data dimensions have already been encoded with axes and position, as on maps, or as the marks on scatter plots. When scatter plots are encoded with different-sized circular marks, they are commonly called bubble graphs (see Figure 5-8#).

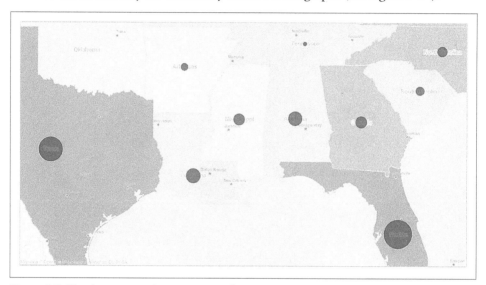

Figure 5-8. Circular areas used to represent and compare quantities per region on a map.

As with other uses of circular area to compare quantity, make sure you are scaling *area*—not radius or diameter—with your data values.

When a fourth dimension needs to be encoded, simple circles or bubbles are replaced with pie graphs. In those cases, each pie's area is meant to be compared with each other whole pie, and each wedge is meant to be compared only within its parent pie. This use of pie graphs dates back to the 19th century, and was pioneered by Playfair and Minard. An example from that era is shown in Figure 5-9.

Bad uses of circles and circular layouts

Circular length and circular bar graphs

The use of circular length is occasionally permissible, as in showing periods of time around a circular clock face. However, that's a rare exception. In almost any other case, the use of circular length a huge "no-no," as are circular bar graphs: they

#Tableau Software Public Gallery. Copyright © 2003–2011 Tableau Software. *http://www.tableausoftware.com/learn/gallery/federal-stimulus-cost*

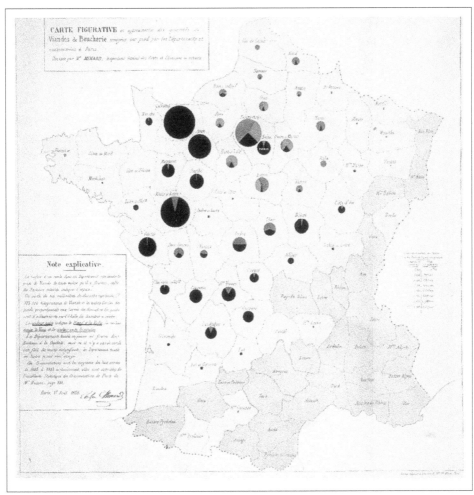

Figure 5-9. Charles Joseph Minard, a French engineer, was one of the first to use pie graphs; this example is from 1858.

create significant distortion of the relative length of the bars. Extracting meaningful comparisons from the data is very difficult under those circumstances. So resist the temptation: just say no. The better approach, as you may have guessed, is to use a plain old, boring, functional, efficient, bar graph.

Pies with many or similarly-sized wedges

If you need precision, or have many fractions/wedges that matter, don't use a pie graph. In those cases, bar graphs with precise labels are a better bet.

Pies for values other than fractions of a whole

We shouldn't have to say this, but we're going to anyway, just to be clear. Pie graphs are *only* for comparing fractions of a whole measure. If you are comparing other quantities—time data, or anything else—no pie for you!

CHAPTER 6

Apply Your Encodings Well

Now that you have a sense of what structure you'll use to represent your data, and how it will be positioned on the page, it's time to consider the other visual properties for encoding your data and to fine-tune your choices.

We'll begin with a discussion of color, including some of the challenges that color selection presents, and the best uses of color. Then we'll review other visual encoding properties—such as size, shape, lines, and text—and give suggestions for how each should be treated. Finally, we'll present some common (and slightly humorous) pitfalls, and give advice for how to avoid them.

Color

Color is tricky. It's very appealing, and as designers, we're tempted to use it all the time. However, getting color right can be much more difficult than it seems.

As discussed in Natural Encodings in Chapter 4, *color is not naturally ordered.*[*] It bears repeating here because it is such a common mistake: avoid using color (hue) for any sort of ranking or ordering of data. You can vary brightness or saturation quite effectively for uses such as heat maps and relative intensity, but please don't vary color as a way to encode rank, order, intensity, or value.

In the defense of color, it can be an excellent property for labeling *categorical* data, or *non-ordered categories* for differentiation purposes. (Examples of non-ordered categories include operating system, gender, region, conference track, and genre.) Just be sure that you don't need too many distinct values if you're using color as the visual property by which to encode categories.

---

[*] No, wavelength and ROYGBIV don't count. Go read the section again.

For help in choosing appropriate color palettes, a great tool is Color-Brewer2.0, at *http://colorbrewer2.org*.

The standard advice for using color to encode categories is to limit your selection to ideally about six—hopefully no more than 12, and absolutely no more than 20—colors and corresponding categories. This will allow you to select colors that are different enough that they can easily be differentiated and clearly named.

The recommended set of 12 colors[†] is shown in Table 6-1.

Table 6-1. It is preferred to use colors from the first half of the list before moving on to the second half.

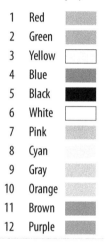

1	Red
2	Green
3	Yellow
4	Blue
5	Black
6	White
7	Pink
8	Cyan
9	Gray
10	Orange
11	Brown
12	Purple

Bear in mind is that the use of color doesn't always help. Use it sparingly and with a specific purpose in mind. Remember that the reader's brain is looking for patterns, and will expect both recurrence itself and the absence of expected recurrence to carry meaning. If you're using color to differentiate categorical data, then you need to let the reader know what the categories are. If the dimension of data you're encoding isn't significant enough to your message to be labeled or explained in some way—or if there *is* no dimension to the data underlying your use of difference colors—then you should limit your use so as not to confuse the reader.

Leverage Common Color Associations

Color may not have a natural ordering, but it does carry a lot of cultural conventions, including many common emotional or aesthetic associations. Some of these include:

[†] Ware, *Information Visualization* (Morgan Kauffman), pp 125–26.

- Red is associated with warning, danger, and warfare. It can also be associated with passion—either love or anger—and blood. In the East it is associated with good luck and prosperity.
- Green is associated with nature, the earth, environmentalism, and renewal. It can also be associated with permission to move ahead, clearance, etc. (as in "green light")—especially when paired with red.
- Yellow is associated with happiness, sunshine, and playfulness. However, on its own or in large fields, it can be irritating. It is also associated with caution.
- Blue is associated with water, coolness, and calm. Depending on the shade, it may be associated with religion or the military.
- Black is associated with mourning and death, but also with luxury and sophistication.
- White is associated with purity, innocence, and weddings, but also with sympathy and the afterlife (and therefore, with death).
- Pink is associated with affection, imagination, and childishness. Light pink is associated with young girls, and light blue with young boys—especially when paired together.
- Grey is associated with neutrality, conservatism, modesty, and maturity.
- Orange is associated with fire, energy, and—in the East—spirituality. It is named for the fruit, and so can also be associated with health and vigor.
- Brown is associated with dirt, leather, stone, and "earthiness." It may also be associated with animal waste.
- Purple is associated with royalty (nobility) and magic (falsehood or artificiality).

Clearly, some of these associations are more desirable than others, and many colors carry associations that are radically different or even directly contrary to each other. You will want to be aware of context and any surrounding visual indicators that may trigger one association rather than another.

See the section on colors under Reader's Context in Chapter 4 for more examples of combinations of colors that carry common associations.

Cognitive Interference and the Stroop Test

Sometimes a color (either the color itself or the perceived meaning of a color) can send a message in direct conflict to a message being sent by the element that color has been applied to (for example, a shape or some text). The reader's brain requires extra time to resolve the disparity, and so there is a delay in understanding and assimilation, an effect known as *cognitive interference*. This is another example of the level of *compatibility* of your encoding, as discussed in Chapter 4.

John Ridley Stroop devised a test to measure this and first published the effect in 1935, in an article entitled "Studies of interference in serial verbal reactions."[‡] Essentially, his experiment consisted of giving participants three lines to read aloud. One line comprised text naming a list of colors ("red, green, yellow, blue") with each word printed in the corresponding color. Another line comprised the same text, with each word printed in a discordant color. The final line comprised no words, but small color swatches, which participants were asked to name (see Figure 6-1). This is now known as the *Stroop Test*.

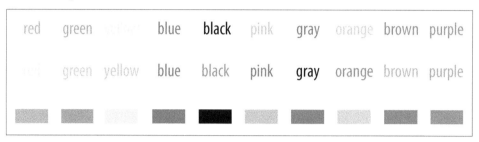

Figure 6-1. A Stroop Test asks the subject to read aloud three different lines, and measures the length of time required to read each one.

Stroop timed how long it took participants to read aloud each of the three lines, and then compared their times. Indeed, the second line nearly universally took the longest to read. This is because the language input (the text of the color name) conflicted with the visual input (the color it was printed in), and the brain needed extra time to resolve the conflict.

It is wise to bear in mind that color has a strong impact on your reader's cognitive load and thought processes; choose your colors accordingly, therefore, to be cooperative with the message you want them to receive so that your communication will be as efficient as possible.

Color Theory

There is a whole wonderful world of color theory out there that is both fascinating and entirely beyond the scope of this short book. We encourage you to learn more about it if you're so inclined; you will reap great rewards in terms of your design savvy. Meanwhile, here are the basics to keep in mind.

There are three main variables when we talk about color: *hue* (the name on the color wheel), *saturation* (a color's purity), and *brightness* (how light or dark the color is).

You can create a monochromatic palette by preserving the hue and adding different amounts of either black or white to vary the brightness (adding black is called *shading* and adding white is called *tinting*). See Figure 6-2 for an example of a monochromatic palette. As we mentioned in Natural Encodings in Chapter 4, these can be very useful for heat maps and encoding relative intensity.

‡ *Journal of Experimental Psychology*, 18, pp 643–662.

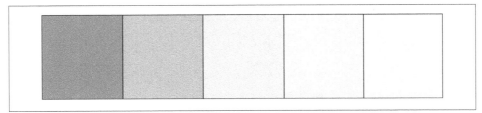

Figure 6-2. Varying shade or tint by adding black or white to a single hue yields a monochromatic palette.

You will likely remember from high school art classes that you can also create color palettes from *complimentary* colors (colors opposite each other on the color wheel), *analogous* colors (neighboring colors from within the same "pie slice" of the color wheel), or *triadic* colors (three colors equally spaced around the color wheel). No matter how you select your group of hues, however, if they all have the same saturation or brightness, they will compete with each other for the eye's attention. Consider playing with shading and tinting until you get a palette that feels pleasing and balanced for your particular needs (see Figure 6-3§).

 Just a reminder that a great resource for help in choosing color palettes friendly to those with color blindness is the Color Laboratory at *http:// colorlab.wickline.org/colorblind/colorlab/*.

Some colors don't go together well. Typically, colors that are far apart on the color wheel (but not perfectly complimentary or triadic) are perceived as conflicting—we would say casually that they "clash." When these hues are of similar brightness (such as red and blue) and are placed next to each other, you sometimes get a "shimmering" effect: your eye doesn't know where to focus first, and can't resolve the discord. This effect can be startling or jarring, so it can grab attention. But it can also make it difficult for the reader to pay attention to the underlying elements or message, so use caution.

Spatial perception of color

Generally speaking, warm colors (reds, oranges, yellows, and browns) will appear to advance to the foreground, and cool colors (greens, blues, purples, and greys) will appear to recede into the background. Similarly, tints (colors with added white) will appear to advance, while shades (colors with added black) will appear to recede. Make use of these natural perceptions to your advantage.

§ Spective® Colour System is the evolved color selection method created by Tony Scauzillo-Golden in 2010 while improving upon existing design industry standard color UIs. Please visit TSG's Spective Productions website (*http://www.spectivepro.com*) for further details. Spective® is registered under United States Patent Reg. No. 3,896,334.

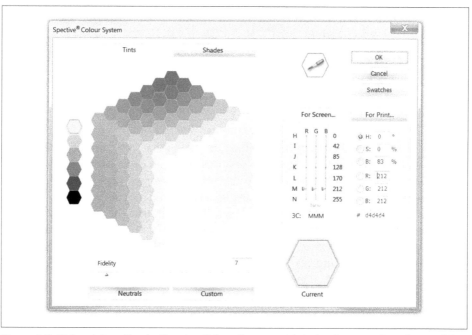

Figure 6-3. Color pickers like the Spective Colour System, with its brightness and resolution sliders as well as standard numerical input fields, can help you select appropriate color palettes.

RGB versus CMYK

Computers and printers use different sets of base colors, or *color spaces*. Computers use RGB (red, green, and blue) while printers use CMYK (cyan, magenta, yellow, and *key*,‖ or black). That's because computers and other light-emitting devices use an *additive color model*, while printers and other ink- or dye-based devices use a *subtractive color model*.

 You may be aware that there are also different ways of modeling the RGB color space: HSV, HSI, and HSL are all based on different geometric alternatives to the standard cube representation. If this leaves you scratching your head, don't worry. You can learn more about them as you interact with various color pickers later on in your journey.

The simple explanation of these two models is as follows. The additive color model uses light to *project* various wavelengths in the spectrum, with red, blue, and green as the primary wavelengths (when you combine all three of these, you get white light). The subtractive color model uses pigments to *absorb* various wavelengths, using cyan,

---

‖ In traditional four-color process printing, each color of ink is rolled onto and printed from a separate plate. Each of the three color plates are *keyed* (aligned) based on the primary plate, which is rolled with black ink.

magenta, and yellow as primaries, and black as the pigment that absorbs all wavelengths. See Figure 6-4, and notice that one model's primary colors are the other model's secondary colors.

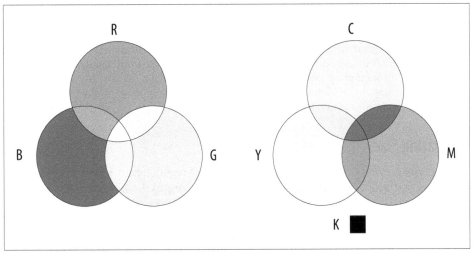

Figure 6-4. The additive color model (RGB) is shown on the left; the subtractive color model (CMYK) is shown on the right.

Design software handles these color spaces differently depending on the expected output. If you know ahead of time where your visualization is destined to be displayed, you can save yourself the headache of converting between the two color spaces by choosing the correct defaults in whatever software or language tool you're working in.

Size

Size can be used to great advantage to represent the relative importance of entities. Even if your larger entity is the same size as others "in reality," making it larger in your visualization makes it more eye-catching and indicates that it is more worthy of attention. You'll see this on organizational charts, where the CEO gets a bigger box, even though the text in the box (or the person it represents) doesn't take up any more physical space than any other job title. Consider using size to draw your reader to central, key, or fundamentally important entities.

Conveying Size

Conveying *relative size* (or *proportion*) accurately can be a challenge, especially for very large (e.g., planets) or very small items (e.g., viruses). You'll often see large items compared to familiar big things: a blue whale, a school bus, the Statue of Liberty, or the Empire State Building. This can be a useful practice if you've got a handy reference item that's near enough in size to the object you'd like to represent. For some fun examples of size comparison, see *http://www.merzo.net/* for (very) big things, and *http://learn.genetics.utah.edu/content/begin/cells/scale/* for (very) small things.

 Sometimes it's not just the entities that matter, but also the relationships among them. Trying to fit the solar system, for example, onto a page, such that the distances between planets remain at scale but the planets don't disappear into tiny dots, may be a challenge. In these kinds of trade-off situations, ask yourself which dimension of the data (the entities or the relationships among them) is most important, and which may be distorted for convenience and accessibility.

Comparing Sizes

We're really good at comparing the surface areas of rectangles in situations where the only thing that's different between them is length. As long as the width remains constant (think: bar graphs and software progress bars), we are very good at guesstimating the relationship of the size of the shapes to each other.

When it comes to rectangles where the width and length both change, we don't judge them as accurately, and we tend to underestimate the differences in size: a square that is 1.4 units long on each side has twice the area of a square with sides of length 1, but doesn't seem "twice as big" (see Figure 6-5). However, compensating for this by scaling length on both axes leads to the opposite problem: disproportionately larger surface areas. The best practice is to scale rectangles by changing only one linear dimension, and to consider using appropriate labels.

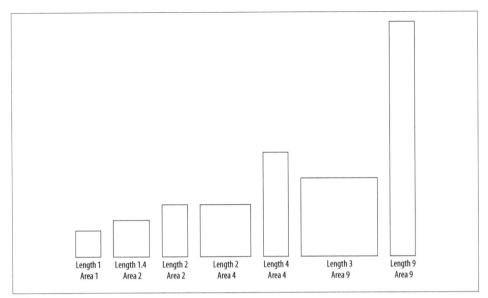

Figure 6-5. *Squares and rectangles of varying edge length and volume.*

We also judge area less well with circles, although, since they are still regular geometric shapes, we can get the general idea. This is why it is so common to encode size and proportion on a graph via the size of the circle (or *bubble*) marking each plotted point. When using circles to represent quantity, make sure you're scaling the surface area and not the diameter/radius/circumference.

 Be careful that on crowded graphs your bubbles don't overlap too much, obscuring each other or labels on the graph. This can make your visualization look amateurish, and frustrate your reader.

Once you get beyond regular geometric shapes into irregular surface areas, all surface-area comparison abilities pretty much go out the window. Consider Figure 6-6, which shows the outlines of two teddy bears to compare the number of toys donated in two consecutive years. A reader might be able to tell that one is bigger than the other, but won't be able to say very accurately by how much.

And in Figure 6-6, which compares the number of dolls donated versus the number of trucks donated, it is nearly impossible to say which silhouette has the larger surface area. These images may be cute or even memorable, but they are not very useful.

Figure 6-6. Comparing irregular surface areas, even within recognizable shapes, is not something our brains are very good at.

Text and Typography

It is very unlikely that you'll come across a helpful visualization that uses no words or numbers of any kind. Most of them do, as titles, axis labels, or other kinds of labels or indicators. So we need to carefully consider which words and numbers are present, how they interact with the visual elements, and what they do or don't say.

Labels are not going to help if the reader can't read them. This may seem obvious, but you'd be amazed at how many visualizations treat words as second-class citizens: they're crammed into spaces where they don't fit, they run over each other or under graphic elements, or they're printed in a font so small that an ant needs a pair of glasses to read them. Here are some ways to ensure your text is effective.

Use Text Sparingly

As with the visual elements in your design, the textual elements you use should be carefully selected and ruthlessly edited: provide only what your reader needs, and no more. This applies to explanatory text, as well as to labels.

For instance, on a graph or chart, you may not need to label every hash mark or your X- and Y-axes. Consider labeling every other hash mark, or only multiples of 5, 10, or

100, or something else appropriate. If the axis labels make clear what the graph measures, then use the title to convey something else, such as the underlying relationship or meaning you hope to convey.

Aside from keeping your visualization clear and clutter-free, a good reason to use text sparingly is that it will lead your reader's eye. Text is an important signal telling your reader's brain how to move through your visualization; if there are words and numbers everywhere, the reader won't know where to begin, or may jump around wildly trying to absorb everything you've written.

Take your reader on a precise, well-planned journey, and don't require him to expend any more brain resources than are necessary to understand your message.

Fonts and Hierarchies

The disagreements over *serif* versus *sans serif* fonts are endless, and unfortunately it is beyond the scope of this book to get into too much detail regarding typography wars. Suffice it to say that many people feel serif fonts (fonts with ornamental shapes at the ends of letters, such as Times, Cambria, or Garamond) are better for setting blocks of text, while sans serif fonts (fonts with clean line endings, such as Helvetica, Arial, or Verdana) are better for titles, tags, and labels.

Remember: your goal is to make things clear and easy to navigate for your reader. So avoid using fancy or trendy fonts just because you can. Stay away from gothic fonts, fantasy fonts, and script fonts. (We're looking at you, Comic Sans.)

Remember that pattern signals meaning: don't change fonts unless you're trying to call the reader's attention to a shift in meaning or category of text. If you really need to include many kinds of titles, labels, or other forms of text, and they just have to have a differentiated look, we suggest you choose a font family with a sufficient number of members of differing weights (such as Regular, Medium, Light, etc.) to encode your categories while preserving a sense of continuity.

For an excellent analysis of creating hierarchy (classes of labels) on maps, we refer you to Justin O'Beirne's excellent posts on "Google Maps & Label Readability" at *http:// herkulano.posterous.com/41latitude-google-maps-label-readability*.

Beware of All Caps

Many of you have no doubt seen the text shown in Figure 6-7, which circulated widely as an email forward around 2003. It was cited in emails as being from a university study (with varying universities cited), though our research has shown an actual citation to be elusive. Still, the example clearly works, since you can, no doubt, read the jumbled text fairly easily.

IT DEOSN'T MTTAER WAHT OREDR THE
LTTEERS IN A WROD ARE, THE OLNY
IPRMOETNT TIHNG IS TAHT THE FRIST AND
LSAT LTTERES ARE AT THE RGHIT PCLAE. THE
RSET CAN BE A TATOL MSES AND YOU CAN
SITLL RAED IT WOUTHIT A PORBELM. TIHS IS
BCUSEAE WE DO NOT RAED ERVEY LTETER
BY IT SLEF BUT THE WROD AS A WLOHE.

Figure 6-8. When the same text is written in all caps, your brain requires more time to process and understand each word.

It deosn't mttaer waht oredr the ltteers in a
wrod are, the olny iprmoetnt tihng is taht
the frist and lsat ltteres are at the rghit pclae.
The rset can be a tatol mses and you can sitll
raed it wouthit a porbelm. Tihs is bcuseae we
do not raed ervey lteter by it slef but the
wrod as a wlohe.

Figure 6-7. The central letters within each word have been jumbled, but the text is still legible.

Now try to read the text in Figure 6-8. You can still do it, but it's harder, right? That's because words have structure, too, and when you print them in all caps you take away much of the visual variation of the letter shapes—particularly the pieces that extend above or below a lower-case *x* (in typography we call these *ascenders* and *descenders*).

Sometimes you will want words and labels to be secondary to other things—lines, shapes, or even other labels—and all caps may be your friend in that instance, since the reader's brain will parse other text more readily, and therefore before parsing the labels in all caps. You can use a combination of form and color (choose lighter, receding shades) to keep the labels subtle.

The bottom line is that shape and structure affect not only the pictorial elements of your visualization, but also the text. Be aware that all caps take the longest to process, and use them with intention.

Avoid Drop Shadows

One of the most horrible ways (because it is so needless) in which to obscure legibility is to add a drop shadow to your text. You have probably seen this done in numerous slide presentations, either in some misguided bid for emphasis or because the presenter was drinking a little too much coffee at 2am. Bottom line: drop shadows on text make your beloved readers cry.

Shape

Shape is a very useful property for labeling or encoding categories. Because of the huge variety of shapes available, and the general ease of differentiating them, shape can be much more evocative than some other properties. The expressive nature of shape has the potential to be both very useful, and very distracting or misleading.

Cultural Connotations

Shape can have *significant* cultural implications: think of the various meanings of crosses, crescents, stars, and shields. One must be extremely careful to not offend the reader or to convey unintended meaning when using shapes. Remember that some readers will not share your assumptions and conventions about shape.

Icons

Icons are a variation of shape. While they tend to have more detail than a simple circle or square, they are initially parsed at a coarse level, and potentially identified by their outlines alone. More detailed examination can reveal additional differentiating factors, but often these are unnecessary. Look, for example, at the outlines of the shapes of tools on a software tool bar, or even at the buttons on most remote controls. The buttons or functions are initially differentiated with shape, even when supported with detail, color, and text.

 When creating icons, consider ways of designing them to be fundamentally different shapes, and select shapes that are evocative of the functions they represent.

Illusions

Beware of the unintended confluence of shapes forming compound images—like seeing ducks or boats in the clouds, our brains look for recognizable shapes in the combination of abstract forms. But some of these may have rude or unfortunate meanings, or simply meanings inappropriate to the tone or subject of your intended message.

Another thing to watch out for is layering. If your visualization gets so crowded that shapes begin to overlap each other, you may cause the illusion of depth where none is intended (an illusion of depth may cause the perception of ranking, with the objects appearing in the "foreground" perceived as more important than those that appear to recede). See Figure 6-9 for an example.

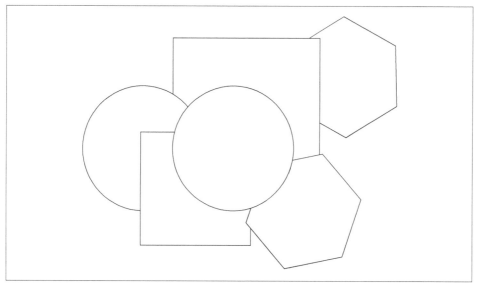

Figure 6-9. Notice how the shapes appear to take on an ordering and respective depth based on how they overlap.

Lines

Lines that connect other entities are excellent for representing all sorts of relationships. They can show many different qualitative factors, as well as quantity or volume of flow. Their visual properties are listed here; examples are shown in Figure 6-10.

Color

    As with most other entities, lines can be colored for categorical or shaded for quantitative meaning.

Weight

    The thickness or boldness of lines can represent magnitude or importance. (Sankey diagrams are built around this metaphor and encoding.) It is difficult for a reader to accurately quantify small differences in line thickness, so it shouldn't be relied upon to encode subtle quantitative differences, unless text labels with quantities are also used.

Endings

    Line endings such as arrows, dots, forked endings, and other shapes can be used to encode different functions of the line, such as source, destination, one-to-many, one direction only, hierarchy, etc.

Pattern

    Lines may be solid, dashed, dotted, or broken in other ways. The density of these patterns may be used to encode quantity, but it's probably safer to use thickness or a label and allow the line pattern to represent qualitative or categorical differences.

Path

Straight, curved, orthogonal, and diagonal line paths can be used to encode different qualities, as well as add metaphorical meaning to the connections that the lines represent.

Taper

Lines that taper from one end to the other can represent direction, relative importance, hierarchy, or other unequal values.

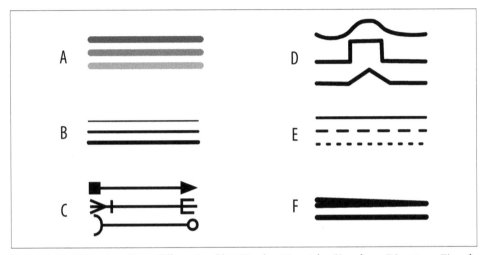

Figure 6-10. Examples of lines differentiated by: A) color; B) weight; C) endings; D) pattern; E) path; F) taper.

When Not to Use Lines

Sometimes the lines that you leave out are just as important as in the ones you include. For a good example of this, see Aaron Koblin's Flight Patterns project at *http://www .aaronkoblin.com/work/flightpatterns/*, which is a visualization of the paths of air traffic over a continent. As you probably know almost right away, it is a map of air traffic over North America. The designer didn't need to include an outline of the country, because there are enough data points to make the shape of the continent clear. The outline would have been superfluous (and may have ended up visually interfering with the data points), so it was omitted.

As always, the goal here is to minimize noise in order to maximize signal. For this reason, the guideline of omission may apply to grid lines, lines that connect entities with their labels, and many other illustrative uses of line. Consider whether the lines you think you need are really necessary. Less can be more.

Keys versus Direct Labeling of Data Points

As a general concept, adding a *key* or *legend* to your visualization seems to make sense. How could there be anything wrong with having legible explanations in an easy-to-find location? A complete key can also serve to show the span of a data dimension, listing all of the categories or ranges of values in one location. How handy!

The potential problem is that having the labels far away from the data imposes an extra cognitive burden on your reader: they can see the data but not decode it until they refocus their attention on the key and look up the appropriate value by dereferencing the encoding. This takes time, can be error-prone, and becomes frustrating when there are many values that need to be decoded.

The alternative suddenly becomes quite attractive: just *directly label* all entities with their values and properties, and you're done. Information at the point of need! No change of focus and no dereferencing required! This must be the superior solution, right?

Well, yes and no. Labels on the data points absolutely make the labeled knowledge more accessible, but only if you can easily read the labels and tell which entities they're attached to. Labels can be obfuscatory if there are a large number of data points located very close together. If the visual density that already exists is compounded by a flock of labels, you haven't improved your clarity at all.

So what's the bottom line? *Context*. It all depends on how many total data points you're dealing with, and how many possible values exist for those data points. Fewer data points or less dense layouts are more likely candidates for direct labeling, because you've got room to add the label text. This is true regardless of the number of values, though more different values benefit from direct labeling, because a key becomes cumbersome when it's got too many values to address. Conversely, a range of fewer possible values, regardless of the number of points, can be well served by a key, because there are fewer values the key has to address.

The trickiest situation is one with many, densely-located data points and many values. In this last situation, direct labels can add visual noise, and a key can become large, unwieldy, and hard to use. Consider, then, labeling only some values, or allowing your reader to turn some or all labels on and off as necessary.

 One set of labels that should always be present is the labels on your axes. These help the reader in a variety of ways; see "Position: Layout and Axes" on page 47.

Pitfalls to Avoid

Communication is the primary goal of data visualization. Any element that hinders— rather than helps—the reader, then, needs to be changed or removed: labels and tags that are in the way, colors that confuse or simply add no value, uncomfortable scales or angles. Each element needs to serve a particular purpose toward the goal of communicating and explaining information. Efficiency matters, because if you're wasting a viewer's time or energy, they're going to move on without receiving your message.

Here are some elements and effects that need to be used judiciously in some cases and avoided at all costs in others. In general, a good rule of thumb for these is: if you're not using these elements for a *very specific reason* (and/or your reason is "they look cool"), then do yourself and your reader a favor and steer clear of them.

3D

It may be tempting to use 3D effects to give your charts and graphs more "oomph," but don't do it unless the dimensions of the data require you to use an extra axis, and you can represent that third dimension in a way that doesn't compromise the other data. If you've got a 3D display, great; otherwise, reconsider. The problem with adding a third dimension to your visualization is that, when presented on a two-dimensional surface, it will add *distortion* (Figure 6-11#). This is visual noise, and will not help your reader even a little bit.

#Jess Bachman (2011). Copyright © 2011, Jess Bachman. *http://www.smarter.org/research/apples-to-oranges/*

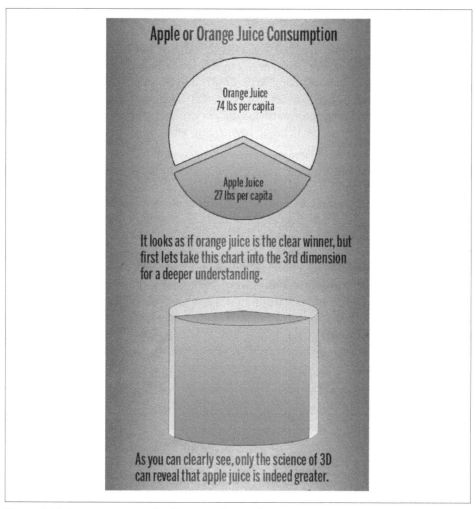

Figure 6-11. An extreme example of how 3D distorts data.

Pies

We discussed this earlier in "Appropriate Use of Circles and Circular Layouts" on page 58, but it bears repeating. Pie graphs are to be reserved for the rare cases in which they are the best way of comparing a few parts of the whole, with very little precision.

Gradients

The problem with gradients is two-fold. First, they add visual noise, by introducing a change where it's not needed. Second, they add a "false" sense of luminance and shadow which may fool the brain into interpreting the luminous region of the gradient as nearer and the darker region as receding. See Figure 6-12 for an interesting example of this.

Not only do darker areas appear to recede, but also assumes the brain a light source comes from above unless otherwise indicated.[*] This creates an interesting effect that will cause top-down gradients to appear "raised" and bottom-up gradients to appear "depressed." Turn the page upside-down, and they seem to switch.

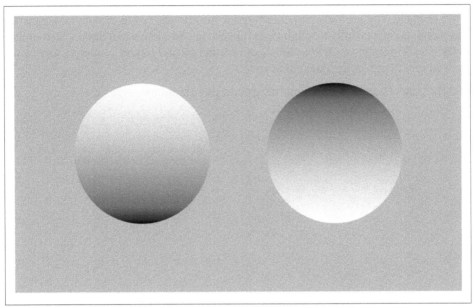

Figure 6-12. Which is the "bump" and which is the "hole"? Turn the image upside down to see them swap.

There are a few situations in which gradients may be helpful, but this is varsity-level design. Unless you know exactly what you're doing, leave gradients alone.

Drop Shadows

Like casual 3D effects, drop shadows applied to text or other figures will only torment your readers by adding visual noise. They may be appropriate in the rare circumstance in which you need to achieve a layering effect or add visual depth to the page. This circumstance will almost never come up for data visualizations; if you feel the need to use this kind of visual effect, you'd better be making an infographic. Even then, tread very carefully.

[*] Ware, *Information Visualization* (Morgan Kauffman), p 246.

Any Excel Defaults

Let's just say it: the Excel defaults are pretty much always wrong. Graph styles, use of 3D, colors, redundant keys and labels: all wrong. Excel has some powerful capabilities, but don't let it make design choices for you. Your message is important enough to warrant your careful consideration and deliberate decision-making.

Conclusion

Well, that's it. You are now prepared to go forth into the world of data and transmit your message successfully through visual encoding and intentional design. Remember to try new things; question your assumptions; iterate and adjust as you go; keep your goals in mind; and let the data guide you.

Embrace the process, and use your newfound powers for awesome!

Additional Resources

Thank you for picking up a copy of *Designing Data Visualizations*! If you're reading this appendix, we hope it means you've already made your way through our compact tome. If so, then you've learned the basics of identifying your goals, selecting appropriate data dimensions to encode, and applying encodings with care. You're ready to implement!

In order to help you do that, here is a list of tools to consider trying, as well as a reading list—these are the books we keep on our shelves and have pored over delightedly or pulled down regularly to help us with tricky design problems and encoding decisions. We hope they serve you well. Happy designing!

Tools

There are myriad tools and language libraries available to help you explore your data or create custom visualizations of it. More appear every day. Here is a partial listing to get you started.

0 to 255 (http://0to255.com/)
> A web-based tool to find darker and lighter variations of colors, in order to make coherent palettes and color schemes. Designed to generate colors that are safe for web use.

Color Brewer 2.0 (http://www.colorbrewer2.com/)
> A web-based tool for generating palettes of colors. Options include the ability to select sequential, diverging, or discrete palettes, as well as number of colors, and hue families. Also allows selection of palettes that are color-blind compatible, photocopier safe, etc.

Color Laboratory (http://colorlab.wickline.org/colorblind/colorlab/)
> This website allows you to select color swatches into a group (or enter custom RGB values) and see how they appear next to one another. You can also simulate how the selected colors are perceived with eight types of color vision deficiency, assuming that you yourself have typical color vision.

D3/ProtoVis (http://mbostock.github.com/d3/, http://mbostock.github.com/protovis/)

D3 is a JavaScript library developed by Michael Bostock. It allows you to bind arbitrary data to a Document Object Model (DOM), and then apply data-driven transformations to the document. D3 is based on ProtoVis, a graphics toolkit developed by Michael Bostock and Jeff Heer that uses JavaScript and SVG for web-native visualizations. ProtoVis is no longer under active development as of September, 2010. Available under the BSD License. Free to use.

ESOM (Emergent, Self-Organizing Maps) (http://databionic-esom.sourceforge.net/index .html)

A suite of programs written in Java and developed by the Databionics Research Group at the University of Marburg, Germany, to perform data mining tasks like clustering, visualization, and classification. Available under the GNU General Public License (GPL).

Fineo (http://www.densitydesign.org/research/fineo/)

A web app for drawing Sankey diagrams and modeling relationships among categorical data. Free to use.

GGobi (http://www.ggobi.org/)

Interactive graphical software for exploring high-dimensional data. It provides dynamic graphic "tours" of the data, as well as scatterplots, barcharts and parallel coordinates plots. Formerly XGobi. Available under the GNU General Public License (GPL).

ggplot2 (http://had.co.nz/ggplot2/)

A plotting toolkit for the R statistics and analysis language. It is based on the grammar of graphics. Available under the GNU General Public License (GPL).

GNUplot (http://www.gnuplot.info/)

A portable, command-line driven graphing utility that can draw using lines, points, boxes, contours, vector fields, surfaces, and various associated text to plot functions and data points in 2D and 3D plots. Free to use.

GraphViz (http://www.graphviz.org/)

Useful for representing structural information as diagrams of abstract graphs and networks, with six different graph formats and many options for colors, fonts, line styles, hyperlinks, and custom shapes. Available under the Eclipse Public License (EPL).

JIT (JavaScript InfoVis Toolkit) (http://thejit.org/)

An open source JavaScript toolkit developed by Nicolas Garcia Belmonte. The website includes a gallery with dozens of examples and the code behind them.

MANET (Missings Are Now Equally Treated) (http://stats.math.uni-augsburg.de/ MANET/)

A suite of graphical tools designed for exploring raw data and studying multivariate features, produced by the RoSuDa group at the University of Augsburg. Specializes in datasets with missing values. Free to use.

Many Eyes (http://www-958.ibm.com/)

A website that lets you visualize data and explore galleries of other people's visualizations to comment, explore, and share. An experimental project from IBM Research and IBM Cognos software group.

Mondrian (http://stats.math.uni-augsburg.de/Mondrian/)

A general-purpose statistical visualization system written in Java and also produced by the RoSuDa group at the University of Augsburg. Particularly useful for working with categorical data, geographical data, and big datasets. Available under the GNU General Public License (GPL).

OmniGraffle (http://www.omnigroup.com/products/omnigraffle/)

The best diagramming tool on MacOS. Easy enough to get started on quickly, with plenty of control available. OmniGraffle also incorporates the GraphViz engine and can import and lay out DOT formatted data files. Many templates and shape stencils available at *http://graffletopia.com/*. Commercial. MacOS only.

OmniGraphSketcher (http://www.omnigroup.com/products/omnigraphsketcher/)

A quick, lightweight, inexpensive tool for sketching graphs. No need to manually draw axes or enter data (though you can)—just start sketching the graph you want. Excellent for ideation and prototyping. Commercial. MacOS only.

OpenDX (http://www.opendx.org/)

An open source tool suite based on IBM's Visualization Data Explorer, it uses a GUI based on X windows and Motif. It can handle overlapping grids, data with non-uniform step sizes, and missing data. Tools include cutting planes, vector line traces, volume rendering, and isosurface/isocontour tools.

Parallel Sets (http://eagereyes.org/parallel-sets)

An exploration tool for categorical data written in Java and developed by Robert Kosara and Caroline Ziemkiewicz. Available under the New BSD License.

Processing (http://processing.org/)

A programming language and development environment initially created by Ben Fry and Casey Reas to serve as a software sketchbook and therefore specifically for working with graphics. It has matured into a powerful tool for creating all kinds of professional visual images. Available under the GNU Lesser GPL.

SCIGraphica (http://scigraphica.sourceforge.net/)

A scientific data visualization package based on Python and C, using the GTK+ and GtkExtra libraries. Available under the GNU General Public Licence (GPL).

Tableau (http://www.tableausoftware.com/)

User-friendly tools that let you drag-and-drop to visualize data and create interactive dashboards. Great for exploring (just please avoid the temptation to just shove it into all your presentations—like all these tools, it is no replacement for thoughtful, custom explanatory design). Commercial with a public version. Windows only.

Wordle (http://www.wordle.net/)

This tool for creating word clouds with adjustable fonts, colors, and layouts was developed by Jonathan Feinberg while at IBM. Great for exploring text-based data (like the Daily Congressional Record or any large corpus), but won't tell the whole story for you. Free to use.

VTK (Visualization Toolkit) (http://www.vtk.org/)

An open source C++ toolkit that supports automated wrapping into Python, Java, and Tcl, developed by Will Schroeder, Ken Martin, and Bill Lorensen. Specializes in 3D computer graphics, modeling, volume rendering, and scientific visualization. Available under the Creative Commons Attribution-NoDerivs 3.0 Unported License.

Reading List

Bertin, Jacques.

Semiology of Graphics: Diagrams, Networks, Maps. ERSI Press: 2010. (Gauthier-Villars: First Edition, 1967—in French.) This foundational classic on the theory of visual communication has recently been re-released, and we recommend you take advantage of its availability if you'd like to get serious about developing solid design chops.

Card, Stuart K., Jock Mackinlay and Ben Shneiderman.

Readings in Information Visualization: Using Vision to Think. Morgan Kaufmann: 1999. The first chapter is recommended. Newer research has supplanted various later portions of the book.

Craig, Malcolm.

Thinking Visually: Business Applications of 14 Core Diagrams. Thomson Learning: 2000. This book is exactly what the title says it is; its scope is limited to diagrams in a business setting. But if that describes what you work with, this is a helpful resource for thinking about context and application.

Few, Stephen.

Show Me the Numbers: Designing Tables and Graphs to Enlighten. Analytics Press: 2004. A beginner-friendly introduction to business presentations and other numerical designs for explanatory visualization.

Information Dashboard Design: The Effective Visual Communication of Data. O'Reilly Media: 2006. This book has strong focus on communicating efficiently and minimizing visual noise. A must-have if you're designing for a Business Intelligence context.

Now You See It: Simple Visualization Techniques for Quantitative Analysis. Analytics Press: 2009. The companion volume to *Show Me the Numbers*, this book focuses on exploratory visualization.

Harris, Robert.
> *Information Graphics: A Comprehensive Illustrated Reference.* Oxford University Press: 2000. A remarkably complete catalog of graph and visualization types. Excellent as a source book for ideas.

Huff, Darrell.
> *How to Lie with Statistics.* WW Norton & Company: 1993. Concise, funny, useful, classic.

Kosslyn, Stephen M.
> *Graph Design for the Eye and Mind.* Oxford University Press: 2006. Excellent and concise book on best practices and cognitive principles for many standard graph types and implementations.

Lipton, Ronnie.
> *The Practical Guide to Information Design.* Wiley: 2007. A wonderfully rich yet simple-to-read text encompassing all kinds of visual properties and how to use them well.

Malamed, Connie.
> *Visual Language for Designers.* Rockport: 2011. A good source for learning about more aspects of graphic design as applied to all kinds of informational visualizations. This book will help take your presentations to the next level.

Norman, Donald A.
> *The Design of Everyday Things.* Basic Books: 2002. A classic, down-to-earth look at practical design for things used by human beings: it takes into account the psychological side of our interaction with everyday objects. Required reading for anyone designing artifacts for other humans to use.

Reas, Casey and Ben Fry.
> *Getting Started with Processing.* O'Reilly Media: 2010. A concise introduction to a programming language specifically created to make visual design simple, written by the language's creators. Appropriate even for those with little programming experience.

Steele, Julie and Noah Iliinsky.
> *Beautiful Visualization.* O'Reilly Media: 2010. A collection of case studies from practitioners working on all kinds of visualization projects. A great (yes, we're biased, but with much gratitude to the wonderful contributors) behind-the-scenes look at decisions and trade-offs made, and the resulting displays.

Tidwell, Jennifer.
> *Designing Interfaces: Patterns for Effective Interaction Design.* O'Reilly Media: Second Edition, 2010. This book focuses on user interface (UI) design, but contains a lot of valuable insight into things like color, visual hierarchies, and alignment. Especially useful if you plan to design interactive visualizations.

Tufte, Edward R.

The Visual Display of Quantitative Information. Graphics Press: Second Edition, 2001. (First Edition, 1983.) Another seminal classic that is as much a design artifact itself as an instructional volume. While many kinds of quantitative data visualizations are treated, there is a focus on statistical graphics.

Envisioning Information. Graphics Press: 1990. Widely regarded as Tufte's best work, this book rewards those who invest time in reading and understanding it, not just flipping through it casually.

Visual Explanations: Images and Quantities, Evidence and Narrative. Graphics Press: 1997. This volume focuses on dynamic data, and contains some compelling and memorable examples, such as the chapter on the Challenger disaster.

Beautiful Evidence. Graphics Press: 2006. It's not necessary to own all four Tufte volumes; much of the key information is repeated. But this one is notable for introducing sparklines.

Ware, Colin.

Information Visualization: Perception for Design. Morgan Kaufmann: Second Edition, 2004. A definitive reference for the understanding of vision, perception, and related cognition. This is the book many visualization professionals turn to when we need to answer fundamental questions of perception.

Visual Thinking for Design. Morgan Kaufmann: 2008. A more concise treatment of visual processing and perception. Not nearly as comprehensive as *Information Visualization*.

Yau, Nathan.

Visualize This: The FlowingData Guide to Design, Visualization, and Statistics. Wiley: 2011. A beginner-friendly book that walks you through both design theory and implementation. It includes ample illustrations and code tutorials that you can reuse and riff on.

Checklist

This Appendix is not meant to replace a full reading of the book. But once you have read it through, this should provide a useful refresher as you work through specific projects.

Determine Your Goals and Supporting Data

- What information need are you attempting to satisfy with this visualization?
- What values or data dimensions are relevant in this context?
- Which of these dimensions matter; matter most; and matter least?
- What are the key relationships that need to be communicated?
- What properties or values may make some individual data points more interesting than the rest?
- What actions might be taken once the reader's information need is satisfied, and what values will justify that action?

Consider Your Reader

- What information does the reader need to be successful?
- How much detail does the reader need?
- How long does the reader have to make any learned information effective?
- What learned or cultural assumptions does the reader have that may affect your design choices?

Select Axes, Layout, and Placement

- Can you encode your most important data dimension or relationship with position?

- Is there a secondary grouping, dimension, or relationship that can be represented spatially? What if you rearrange or invert groupings?
- Does your direction make sense? Where does the data begin and end? Where should the reader start reading? Which way to the relationships flow?
- Does the placement of your entities reflect their relationships to each other?
- Does the placement of your entities reflect their relationship to reality?

Evaluate Your Encoding Entities

- Are you using conventional encodings and formats? If not, are you sure you have something better?
- Are you using color to represent quantity? Stop it. Use size or placement instead.
- Are your shapes, colors, icons, and text evocative of the properties that exist and that you want to communicate?
- Are you using the same visual encoding for more than one data dimension? Try to pick another one.
- Are you using extra visual properties to redundantly encode your data? Good job!

Reveal the Data's Relationships

- Are the most important relationships revealed?
- Do the relationships need to be called out with links or labels? Or a specific flag?
- Are all the displayed relationships actually relevant and useful?
- Are you redundantly encoding your links?

Choose Titles, Tags, and Labels

- Is the reader from within your industry or outside of it? What about other readers outside of the core audience group? Consider how this will affect your vocabulary choices.
- Is it worth using an industry term for the sake of precision (knowing that the reader may have to look it up), or would a lay term work just as well?
- Will the reader be able to decipher any unknown terms from context, or will a vocabulary gap obscure the meaning of all or part of the information presented?
- Is everything important labeled? Are all of your labels necessary?
- Is your key or legend necessary? Is it ordered in a useful way?

Analyze Patterns and Consistency

- Have you been consistent in membership, ordering, placement, and other encodings?
- Things that are the same should look the same. Is that so?
- Things that are different should look different. Is that so?

About the Authors

Noah Iliinsky has spent the last several years thinking about effective approaches to creating information visualizations. He also works in interface and interaction design, all from a functional and user-centered perspective. Before becoming a designer, he was a programmer for several years. He has a master's degree in technical communication from the University of Washington, and a bachelor's degree in physics from Reed College.

Julie Steele has been working in freelance graphic design since she was 14 years old. She finds beauty in discovering new ways to understand and think about complex systems, and so enjoys applying visual principles to the challenge of visualizing data. She is also an editor at O'Reilly Media. She holds a master's degree in political science (international relations) from Rutgers University, and a bachelor's degree in English from Calvin College.

Have it your way.

Get even more for your money.

Join the O'Reilly Community, and register the O'Reilly books you own. It's free, and you'll get:

- $4.99 ebook upgrade offer
- 40% upgrade offer on O'Reilly print books
- Membership discounts on books and events
- Free lifetime updates to ebooks and videos
- Multiple ebook formats, DRM FREE
- Participation in the O'Reilly community
- Newsletters
- Account management
- 100% Satisfaction Guarantee

Signing up is easy:

1. **Go to: oreilly.com/go/register**
2. **Create an O'Reilly login.**
3. **Provide your address.**
4. **Register your books.**

Note: English-language books only

To order books online:
oreilly.com/store

For questions about products or an order:
orders@oreilly.com

To sign up to get topic-specific email announcements and/or news about upcoming books, conferences, special offers, and new technologies:
elists@oreilly.com

For technical questions about book content:
booktech@oreilly.com

To submit new book proposals to our editors:
proposals@oreilly.com

O'Reilly books are available in multiple DRM-free ebook formats. For more information:
oreilly.com/ebooks

O'REILLY®

Spreading the knowledge of innovators   oreilly.com

Milton Keynes UK
Ingram Content Group UK Ltd.
UKHW011432310824
447677UK00007B/175